ZIP Bible

Istok Kespret

DATA BECKER
EDITION

Abacus

Copyright © 1996   **Abacus**
                          5370 52nd Street SE
                          Grand Rapids, MI 49512

Copyright © 1996   **Data Becker, GmbH**
                          Merowingerstrasse 30

                          40223 Duesseldorf, Germany

Credits	
Managing Editor	Scott Slaughter
Editors	Louise Benzer, Paul Benson, Scott Slaughter
Technical Reviewers	Jim Oldfield, Jr., Paul A. Benson, Gene Traas, George Miller
Language Specialist	Al Wier
Layout Editor	Scott Slaughter
CD-ROM Engineer	Paul A. Benson
Cover Art & Design	Melinda Thede

Printed in the U.S.A.

ISBN 1-55755-305-X

10 9 8 7 6 5 4 3 2

Table Of Contents

1. Data Compression   1

2. Data Compression Elements   25

3. Decompressing Data   33

4. Compressing Your Data 61

7. EXE Compressors   161

8. Command Summary And Switches   187

9. Installing The Companion CD-ROM   245

10. Glossary Of Terms   251

Index   257

The Zip Bible Companion CD-ROM

Thank you for purchasing **The ZIP Bible**. We hope this book will be an indispensable reference guide to archiving your files. The companion CD-ROM contains dozens of practical utilities for zipping and unzipping all files.

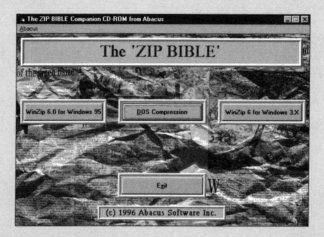

Installing The Companion CD-ROM

DOS

Insert the companion CD into your CD-ROM drive. Log to that drive and type the following:

`install` `Enter`

and follow the instructions.

Windows

Windows users type:

`menu` `Enter`

and follow the instructions.

See Chapter 9 for complete installation instructions.

Data Compression

1

Introduction To Data Compression Programs

Even if you're not aware of it, you've probably already used some type of data compression. Fax machines have been compressing data for years. Microsoft, Borland, Lotus, Novell and most other major software publishers use data compression for distributing the programs included in their software packages. If you've ever used the Internet, CompuServe, Prodigy, America OnLine or other online services, then you've probably used data compression to download files to your PC.

This book explains data compression in general. We won't focus on a particular program. Instead, we'll explain how and what to compress and how to retrieve your data. You'll also find information about the advanced features of data compression programs. This information will help you get the most from your compression program.

We've also included information on all the parameters and options of the data compression programs discussed in this book. Since you probably aren't familiar with all the programs introduced in this book, you'll have a chance to see what these programs have to offer. For example, you may find that another program works faster or is easier to run.

The term "data compression" may be new. However, maybe you've heard some of the other terms used for data compression such as zipping, compressing, packing, squeezing, squashing or crunching. The term "zipping" is now a generic term used for all data compression. The word "archive" is another example of a generic term is used as a noun or verb. Archives can be a collection of compressed files or "zipped" files. Also, an archive can itself be a compressed file. Archiving is also the same as "zipping."

Data compression utilities and programs

Several data compression programs are available. Many of these programs were available first as shareware. These programs are usually well worth their low price. This is especially true since most software companies distribute their programs in compressed

1

form. These companies often use some variation of these shareware programs as part of their installation procedure. This is one reason why data compression programs are so popular.

Users have demanded more storage space since first computer was released. Fortunately, today we have data compression utilities. Most of the writers of these utilities have tackled the compression problems differently. That is, each program has its own "compression algorithm."

Several books have been published over the years praising various methods and disciplines of compressing data files. Each author has their own "method" or algorithm for compression. These algorithms are usually patented. We'll discuss the methods and theory of compressing data later in this chapter.

Although the concept of data compression was originally developed to make data communication more cost effective, it has become extremely useful for both software developers and users.

Uses for data compression programs

There's a growing preoccupation with online services and the Internet. Many users transfer or *download* files from an online service or Internet site to their personal computer. The charges for the online service is usually based on the amount of time the user is connected to the service. Therefore, zipping or compressing the files reduces the transfer time. This, in turn, reduces the monthly charges.

Data compression lowers the cost of passing data from one medium to another. So you can send and receive information more economically. Data compression is also useful when you back up your hard drive because fewer tapes or diskettes are needed.

Why data compression programs are used

Like most users, you probably think that the data on your PC requires too much hard drive space. Data compression programs make it possible to reduce the amount of space your data requires. For some types of data, a typical data compression program can decrease the required amount of disk space by 50% to 90%. Although hard drive prices have dropped to about 50 cents per Meg, you never have too much hard drive space. You probably have some old files on your hard drive that you seldom use but don't want to delete. To conserve hard drive space, you can compress the files until you need them. Later, when you want something from that archive, you can quickly decompress them.

Clipart is another example of what you may have on your drive and want to compress. Clipart usually requires a lot of precious space. Since you may need an image only occasionally, use a data compression utility to create a clipart archive instead of keeping them on your drive "exploded." You'll be surprised how much valuable space you'll regain on your hard drive.

If you connect to one of the many bulletin boards using a modem, you can decrease telephone charges by compressing files. Also, a compressed file can be transferred much faster than an uncompressed file. So, bulletin board systems have also played a major role in the spread of data compression programs. Most of the popular data compression programs are available directly from the bulletin board.

It's relatively easy to compress and decompress data. Recently the number of data compression programs has dramatically increased. Also, the range of functions in these programs has increased over the years.

Today, some data compression programs can be used as backup systems (such as Zip Drives), can write one archive to several diskettes, and can process directory trees node by node. You can even find data compression programs that use 80486 and Pentium processors and special types of memory.

Let's say you have 12 monthly reports for the year that you would like to send to a fellow worker some distance away (say, Zanzibar). You can copy each report onto a diskette each as a separate file: Janrep, Febrep, Marrep, Aprrep,.....etc. Alternatively, you can combine all twelve of the reports into a single 1996rep.zip file and then copy this file to the diskette. The result is less apparent clutter when the diskette arrives in Zanzibar.

The zipped file will still contain the 12 individual reports. The only difference is that they'll seem more organized. Then your fellow worker can unzip 1996rep.zip and they magically appear in Zanzibar.

You can zip files combined from different directories and even zip huge files that span more than one floppy diskette. We'll show you how later.

Why data must be compressed

Eventually, most computer users discover that they don't have enough hard drive space for all their data and programs. One way to solve this problem is to buy a second hard drive. However, it seems that the more hard drive space you have, the more you need. Another solution is to back up (temporarily store) data you're not using on diskettes. Unfortunately, doing this can be time-consuming.

As we mentioned, users who send data over telephone lines with a modem were the first ones to use data compression programs. Since each minute saved during data transfer saved money, data compression became very important for these users.

Now other computer users are looking for ways to minimize the amount of data transferred not only over telephone lines, but also to external media, such as floppy diskettes. Backing up the data even on a modest sized hard drive can require dozens of floppy diskettes. However, a program that compresses data can significantly reduce the number of floppy diskettes needed.

There are also ways to reduce the amount of space for data on the hard drive. Modern hard drives use a storage method that yields a higher capacity in the same amount of space than hard drives that use other coding methods. Although the hardware already codes and optimizes the data, there are transparent data compression programs, such as Stacker or DoubleSpace, that achieve an even higher increase in storage capacity.

Advantages of data compression programs

Therefore, many programs devoted exclusively to data compression and decompression have been created. Compared to their hardware counterparts, in which special chips in the PC perform data compression, software data compression programs have obvious advantages:

Flexibility

Since it's software, a data compression program can be quickly adapted as new developments and improvements in data compression algorithms become available.

Low cost

As you know, hardware is expensive. Because the majority of data compression programs are available as public domain software or shareware, they are more affordable than purchasing new hardware.

Within a short time period, dozens of data compression programs have appeared. Some of the most popular ones are PKZIP, LHARC, ARJ, and LZEXE. Also, many data compression programs are continuously being improved.

Many data compression programs are distributed as shareware. The authors request payment of a specific fee in return for granting you the right to use the program. If you benefit from any shareware programs, register with the author of the program and send him/her the fee they deserve. It's worth your time because the programmer will be motivated to improve and polish his or her product.

> The programs ICE, LHARC, and LHA are from the same developer and follow one another in chronological order. LHARC is one of the classic data compression programs. In this book, we'll base our discussion on the newest version, LHA 2.13. The differences between this version and the older versions mainly involve the enhanced options.

Overview Of Data Compression

This book won't include a lot of technical information. Therefore, we won't discuss the latest modifications of compression algorithms. We wrote this book for the average computer user who wants to know more about data compression.

We'll begin with a summary of data compression. This will help you understand the basics of this process.

Types of compression

The type of data compression you use mainly depends on the type of file you want to compress. If a file contains various types of information, it's more difficult to compress the file. For example, let's look at the following file. It shows only the following information when we display it at the DOS prompt using the DIR command:

```
DIR BIG.DAT
```

```
C:\EXAMPLE>dir

 Volume in drive C is C_DRIVE
 Volume Serial Number is 201A-1EE9
 Directory of C:\EXAMPLE

.              <DIR>         12-08-95   4:52a .
..             <DIR>         12-08-95   4:52a ..
BIG      DAT        1,760   01-03-96  10:45a big.dat
        1 file(s)            1,760 bytes
        2 dir(s)       440,696,832 bytes free

C:\EXAMPLE>
```

In this example, we have a file named BIG.DAT. It's 1,760 characters in size. This isn't a large file considering that this hard drive has 440 Meg free. If we display the file by entering

```
TYPE BIG.DAT
```

the following appears on the screen:

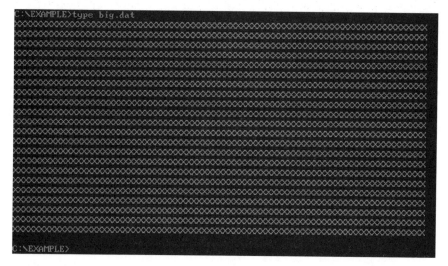

As you can see, this file is simply a sequence of 1,716 "x"s. Instead of wasting all this space by storing all the "x"s separately, we can simply store the number of "x"s. By doing this, we can reduce the file information to a compact form:

```
TYPE SMALL.DAT
x1716
```

Only 5 bytes are needed to save BIG.DAT in a compressed form. This results in a compression ratio of more than 1% of the original size of the file.

According to this method, a file is arranged according to the frequency of specific characters. A table records how often a specific character appears in the file. So, the principle of "X1188" is simply taken one step further.

You may think that you couldn't use this method to compress any of your files. Even if there were such files, they would probably be nonsensical like our example. Obviously, there aren't very many words with long enough sequences of the same letter. For example, we could reduce the nonsensical word "Millleader" using this method to the following:

```
MI3LEADER
```

As you can see, we saved only one character. This example also clearly shows this compression method isn't suitable for text files. However, this method is suitable for *graphic files*. PCs must process an enormous amount of graphic data. Some very complex algorithms are used to reduce the gigantic flow of data in graphic files. A popular format for storing graphics is called the PCX format. Windows Paintbrush uses PCX files.

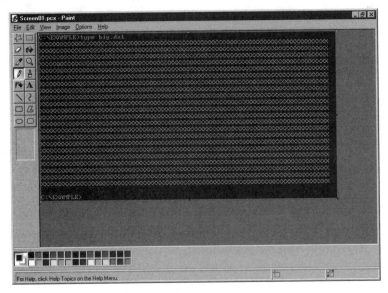

The DOS screen as a PCX file

7

As you can see in the above illustration, a program made a "snapshot" of the DOS screen and then converted it into PCX graphics format. Much of the graphics information in the figure appears more than once. Therefore, it would be a waste of memory space if each dot on the screen were assigned a corresponding 1:1 information ratio in the file.

With a resolution of 2,000 characters on a normal text screen and a VGA resolution of 9 x 16 dots per character, 288,000 dots of information must be stored in black and white. If the graphic is in color, then various color mixtures per dot are added. The information requirements are increased significantly. However, if you look at the actual size of the file, you'll see that it isn't very large.

As you can see, the size of the file has been drastically reduced. We used the method we just discussed to do this. We'll show you a small portion of this FIGURE.PCX file and explain it to you. For example, three byte combinations occur frequently:

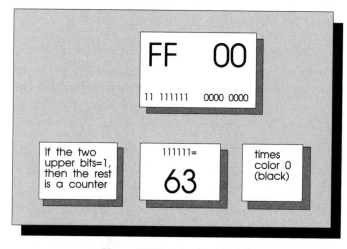

How a PCX entry is encoded

The FF 00 entry is compressed. The secret is in the top two bits (bits 6 and 7) of the first byte. If both of these bits are set, then the remaining 6 bits are a repetition factor. Since all the remaining bits are set, the factor is 63.

The color information of the next byte (00, or black) is repeated 63 times as a dot of the graphic. If the first two bits weren't 11, the rest of the byte would have to be interpreted as direct color code of a single graphic dot.

Reducing text files

As we've explained, a simple method of repetition counting won't work when the data is thoroughly mixed. Text files are an example. To determine an appropriate compression method for these types of files, first you must understand how files and data are stored.

ASCII (American Standard Code for Information Interchange) is the standard code for data in the PC world. ASCII specifies that all existing characters in the PC are assigned a specific code. This standardization makes it possible for information to be exchanged between different data processing systems. The ASCII code specifies a manageable length of a byte. Since a byte can take on 256 different combinations, 256 characters are possible.

Perhaps you think 256 characters sounds like too many, considering that there are only 26 letters in the alphabet. However, these characters also include the 10 numerals, punctuation marks, and foreign characters. Graphic symbols, which create borders and lines on the screen in windows and dialog boxes, are also included. ASCII also includes the invisible characters that tell the printer to print in bold, italics, etc.; these characters are called printer control codes. All of these codes come under the category of ASCII characters. Three groups of character codes are available:

ASCII Code	Code group
0-31	Control characters
32-173	Text characters
174-255	Graphic characters

Basically, every file is an ASCII file because all the codes stored in the file are stored according to the ASCII standard (although there are some exceptions). An ASCII file is a text file in the narrowest definition of ASCII. This type of file contains only information that can be read.

Now let's try to compress an ASCII file. Let's assume that a text file should use only codes 32 to 127. Now, if all the characters use a code that is less than 128, you won't need bit 8 of the ASCII code. This is possible because one character or byte consists of 8 bits. A bit can take on one of two values: Either the value 1 or the value 0.

```
0000 0000 = 0 (all bits are 0)
0000 0001 = 1
0000 0010 = 2
...
...
0111 1111 = 127 (only bit 8 is 0)
...
1111 1110 = 254
1111 1111 = 255 (all bits are 1)
```

So, only 7 bits are needed to represent 128 different combinations. This is enough for all the codes of text files. The far left digit of the byte, bit 8, is always 0 for text codes.

It's possible to create a method for converting or encoding the 7-bit code into 8-bit bytes. This would be another method of data compression.

The following illustration shows the idea behind this compression method. First, each letter of the word is assigned the corresponding ASCII code. To better represent the compression process, the code is represented as a binary number instead of a decimal number (i.e., the code consists of the appropriate combination of ones and zeros).

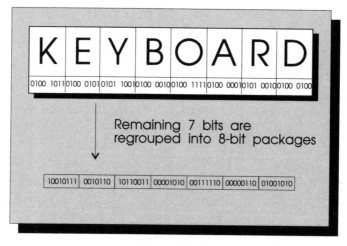

The word "KEYBOARD" being compressed

Next, the data is compressed. To do this, we ignore the eighth (far left) bit of all the characters (since it is always zero). The remaining seven bits give us a chain of 56 ones and zeros (8 letters x 7 bits). These are now regrouped into 8-bit packages and stored.

The file is now reduced to one eighth of the original size. As a result, we've encoded the original file. Using an ASCII table, you can determine which characters replace the word "KEYBOARD" in the file.

To restore such a file to its original state, simply extract seven bits at a time until the file is restored. To restore the original character, insert a 0 at the far left position of each group of seven bits (bit 8).

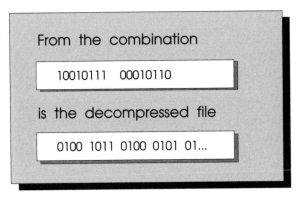

From the combination

10010111   00010110

is the decompressed file

0100 1011 0100 0101 01...

Decompression is compression in reverse

Data Compression In Detail

As you've seen in the "Overview Of Data Compression" section, it's possible to make files smaller. However, you're probably not impressed by a compression method that saves only 12.5% (one-eighth) of your disk space.

We used text (ASCII) files as an example in the "Overview Of Data Compression" section because the method won't work on program files. Unlike text files, you cannot assume that the eighth bit of the data bytes will always be 0 with program files. So, you must use a completely different method for nontext files.

How does this method work?

Remember, a byte consists of eight bits. So, each byte can represent one of 256 different values and, therefore, up to 256 characters.

Now we must determine how to compress a file that contains all 256 characters. All eight bits are needed to store the character as an ASCII code. If one bit is missing, the character cannot be reconstructed.

One solution is to assign a short code to the frequently-used characters and assign a longer code to the characters that are rarely used. This doesn't necessarily involve counting letters and using statistical data to change the ASCII codes yourself. Although you won't change the ASCII code, you can create other bit combinations to recode various characters.

Huffman method

This is exactly what the Huffman method of data compression does. By assigning short bit patterns to the most frequently-used characters and long bit patterns to the less frequently used characters, you can decrease the length of the characters below the default length of eight bits.

This method isn't a recent development. Instead, it's a mathematically-based analysis from the 1950s. This method is so safe that all fax devices use a variation based on the Huffman algorithm to compress and transmit information.

Most data compression programs are derived from a Huffman algorithm that is usually modified. Such methods are usually called *squeezing*. With this method, the type of code is irrelevant whether it's from the entire ASCII spectrum or whether the characters are even ASCII characters.

Instead, you must determine the frequency of the characters being encoded. From the results of these frequency tests, the new bit patterns are formed. So, the Huffman algorithm consists of two steps:

1. Determining the number of times (frequency) each character appears in a file.

2. Creating an encoding scheme based on the frequency of each character.

We'll use an example to devise an encoding scheme to compress a file using the Huffman method.

To demonstrate this method, we can use a file of any size with any contents. For this example we'll use a file called TEST.DAT. We could have also used a large executable file (a spreadsheet program with more than 600,000 bytes) or a large name and address file with hundreds of thousands of entries.

Chapter 1

The following appears when we display the directory on our hard drive for this file:

```
C:\EXAMPLE>dir

 Volume in drive C is C_DRIVE
 Volume Serial Number is 201A-1EE9
 Directory of C:\EXAMPLE

.            <DIR>          12-08-95   4:52a .
..           <DIR>          12-08-95   4:52a ..
TEST     DAT              160 01-03-96 11:20a TEST.DAT
         1 file(s)              160 bytes
         2 dir(s)      435,519,488 bytes free

C:\EXAMPLE>
```

TEST.DAT is 160 bytes long. This is large enough for our example but the file could also be any other size.

The contents of the file are more important than the size of the file for the Huffman algorithm. First, we must count all the different characters contained in the file. The following illustration shows the results:

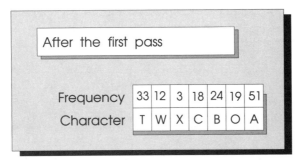

After the first pass

Frequency	33	12	3	18	24	19	51
Character	T	W	X	C	B	O	A

Counting characters in TEST.DAT

Although we don't know the purpose of the file, we do know the file contains only the letters T, W, X, C, B, O, and A. The sequence of the characters in the file isn't important for the compression method. The way the letters in the figure are arranged isn't important either. The table is arranged like this only to make it easier to see the codes in the figures.

Structure of the new codes

Remember our rule for encoding characters: The most frequently used characters have short codes, while the least frequently used characters have long codes.

First, we'll choose the two characters that appear least frequently in the file. From the above figure, you can see that these characters are "X", which appears 3 times, and "W", which appears 12 times. Both characters are "combined" to form a node. The contents of this node are the sum of both frequencies, 3 + 12 = 15.

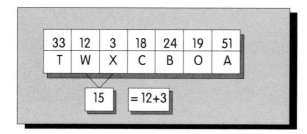

The first node

At this point, we're no longer concerned with the two original values (12 and 3). Instead, we'll include the contents of this node as we search for the next pair of characters with the lowest frequencies. This time we find the letter "C", which appears 18 times, and the node made up of W and X appears 15 times. As a result, we have a new node consisting of this node pair with a combined value of 33.

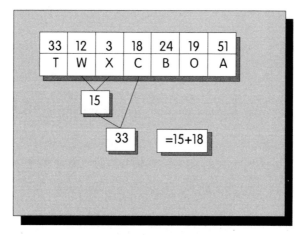

Finding the second node

As you can see, this procedure is actually rather simple. Notice that the value 33 appears twice. However, this isn't a problem.

Continue this method of finding the least frequently used node. When there are no more pairs left to compare, you've reached the bottom (or first) node. This is called the root or anchor, because it's only possible to enter this treelike structure through the root.

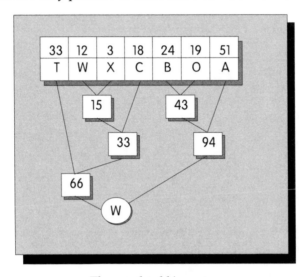

The completed binary tree

The tree structure created by repeatedly searching for the smallest value pairs is important to the computer world. This structure is also called a binary tree, because there are a maximum of two branching options from each node.

Now we must determine how to use this binary tree to create an encoding scheme to compress our data. As you can see, there are only two ways to leave a node. Also remember that a bit can have only two values (zero or one).

The next step is to start at the root, and at each node decide whether you should move in the direction of the left or right character. If you move to the left of the node, then you will encode a zero; if you move to the right of the node, you'll encode a one. When you reach the top branch, you've completed the encoding scheme for the file.

The following steps are needed for the letter "T":

- ❖ Start at the root

- ❖ **Left(0)** to node 66

- ❖ **Left(0)** to "T"

- ❖ New code —> **00**

Use the same procedure for the long path to the "X":

- ❖ Start at the root

- ❖ **Left(0)** to node 66

- ❖ **Right(1)** to node 33

- ❖ **Left(0)** to node 15

- ❖ **Right(1)** to target "X"

- ❖ New code is **0101**

The following illustration shows the new codes and provides an overview of all the paths from the root to the target letter.

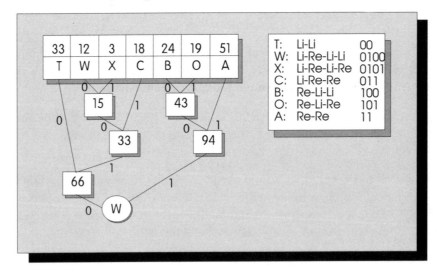

How space is saved

As you can see in the previous figure, characters that occur frequently, such as "A" or "T", receive short 2 bit codes, while characters that don't occur frequently (W or X) have longer 4 bit codes.

You can easily determine the compression ratio.

The original file, TEST.DAT, consists of 160 characters.

❖ 160 characters x 8 bits = 1,280 bits

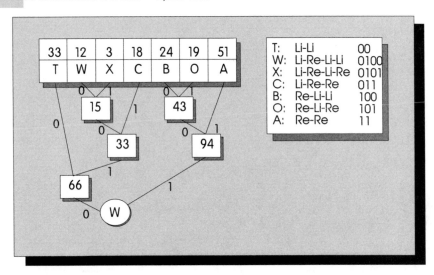

Determining the new codes

The calculation for the new file, called TEST.CMP, look as follows:

From the original 1,290 bits, we now have 411. With this method, the file was compressed to 32% of its original size.

After determining the codes, the program must run through the entire file a second time. This time, the program reads every character and replaces it with its shortened code. It's also important to save the code tree in the file. The only way to decompress the compressed file is to use this tree. However, this decreases the compression ratio, because the tree also requires disk space.

As you can see, you must be very careful when you compress and decompress files. If even the smallest bit in the file is lost or set incorrectly (0 instead 1), then the file will probably be worthless.

Comparing Compression Programs

Now that you know the theory behind compression methods, we'll discuss which programs are best suited for compressing certain files.

Testing the compression programs

To determine which compression program should be used with specific files, we performed some experiments using the following hardware:

- 486/66

- 170 HD hard drive

- 8 Meg of RAM

You should be able to reproduce similar results on your computer system. However, remember that as the quality of the hardware increases, so does the speed of the data compression program.

Test results

The following tables show which compression programs work best with which files. We tested the following programs:

- ARJ 2.41

- LHA 2.13

- PKZIP 2.04g

- ZOO 2.10

We used the latest versions of the compression programs for the tests. We also had SMARTDRV.EXE running on the computer. SMARTDRV.EXE is available with MS-DOS Version 5 and higher. The computer used to test the compression programs was a DX2/66 so your system may produce different results. You'll find more detailed descriptions of the programs later that we tested.

It's interesting to study the compression ratios achieved by compression programs with different types of files. As you may have realized when we introduced the data compression algorithms, the type of file plays an important role in which compression method is used.

The following are the most frequently used and important file types:

File type	Amount of data
Text file	291,262 bytes
dBASE files	860,970 bytes
DOS program	309,696 bytes
Windows program Help files	1,914,880 bytes
PCX graphic file	1,278,248 bytes
TIF graphic file	1,228,546 bytes

"Amount of data" indicates the size of all the files that the programs archived.

Type	ARJ	LHA	PKZIP	ZOO
Text file	28.1	31	27	42
dBASE file	16.5	17	16	20
DOS program	45.7	47	45	64
Windows program Help file	84.1	86	83	0
PCX file	79.6	81	79	86
TIF file	96.3	96	96	0

The file size after compression is specified in percentages. PKZIP had the best data compression with 27%. We chose the default settings for all the programs.

The compression times are almost as important as the compression ratios. The following figures were achieved by data compression programs running without a cache program:

19

Type	ARJ	LHA	PKZIP	ZOO
Text file	0:08	0:09	0:04	0:05
dBASE file	0:14	0:25	0:08	0:12
DOS program	0:09	0:09	0:05	0:07
Windows program Help file	0:53	0:51	0:41	1:31
PCX file	0:35	0:39	0:25	0:41
TIF file	0:34	0:33	0:30	1:08

PKZIP and ARJ have switches that let you control the kind of compression as well as the time. However, a better compression ratio always slows down compression time (and vice versa).

What do the results mean?

Now we must determine what all these values mean. The following column chart, which contains the information from the table, may help you understand the results.

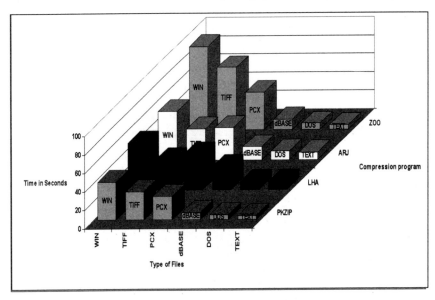

Summary of compression ratios

As you've probably already realized, text files (or text-like files) can be compressed the most. The compression programs PKZIP, LHA, and ARJ can compress text files to about 27% of their original size.

Compressing binary files results in very different compression ratios. DOS programs compress to about half their original size, while Windows programs compress to less than half. This is strange, considering the compression times. Despite search times for Windows programs that are much longer, the compression ratio for Windows programs is lower than the compression ratio for DOS programs.

This indicates that Windows programs are structured differently than normal DOS programs. We'll discuss this in more detail later in Chapter 7. Windows programs are structured so differently that these special compression programs (EXE compression programs) refuse to work.

We were surprised by ARJ's compression time. This program required 1 minute and 31 seconds (91 seconds) to compress the same data that LHA compressed in about half that time. PKZIP took less than one third the time. Although you may think that ARJ takes longer because it's so thorough and produces the best compression, this isn't the case.

```
C:\>arj a graphics *.pcx *.tif *.bmp
ARJ 2.41a Copyright (c) 1990-93 Robert K Jung. Jul 10 1993
*** This SHAREWARE program is NOT REGISTERED for use in a business, commercial,
*** government, or institutional environment except for evaluation purposes.

Creating archive  : GRAPHICS.ARJ
Adding     SAMPLE.PCX     79.6%
Adding     SAMPLE.TIF     96.3%
Adding     JD.BMP         74.5%
Adding     SAMPLE.BMP     59.4%
    4 file(s)

C:\>
```

Poor compression ratios

Certain files, for example TIF, BMP and PCX graphic files, are more difficult to compress than other files. While you can reduce TIF files to 96% of their original size, it's not unusual to see compression ratios from 0 to 96% for other graphic files.

Even ARJ, which is usually so thorough, provides only mediocre results. This occurs because some files, such as these graphic files, are already compressed. The image information is compressed very cleverly to keep memory requirements within limits.

Therefore, continually compressing a file to reduce it to the ideal size of one byte simply doesn't work. Even repeating the compression procedure once on a compressed file is useless because the contents of the file are already optimized.

You're probably wondering why some files that are already compressed and (presumably) optimized still produce a compression ratio of 1%. This occurs because every archive file also needs uncompressed data, such as file and pathnames, the coding tree (explained earlier in this chapter), and some other statistical data. Although it's possible to compress some of this data, later the program will create another coding tree, which creates more statistical data, etc.

Also, repeatedly compressing data is dangerous. The more often you compress a file, the more alienated the contents become. Although this isn't dangerous by itself, compressed data is prone to defects. One error in a file that has been compressed once isn't too bad. In this case, usually one defective file of the archive will be lost. However, if you have a file that has been compressed more than once, one error will probably damage the entire archive.

Using a cache program

To increase compression times of the compression tests, we used a cache program. This type of program monitors the data traffic between the hard drive and PC and temporarily stores data in RAM. The next time the data is accessed, you won't use the hard drive. Instead, you'll get the data from RAM, which is much faster.

Many people use cache programs without even knowing it. For example , you probably have a program called SMARTDRV.EXE if you use Windows in one of your system files (CONFIG.SYS or AUTOEXEC.BAT). Other examples of cache programs include NCACHE.EXE from Norton Utilities or QEMM.

Look at both your AUTOEXEC.BAT and CONFIG.SYS files. Many computer users don't know what is in these files. As a result, sometimes these users have all three of these programs running on their computers. Unfortunately, this doesn't mean that their computers run three times as fast. Actually the opposite is true. Therefore, it's important that you choose only one cache program. When you use a cache program, the compression times for the same data decrease.

Obviously, all compression programs benefit from working with cache programs, but the increase in speed isn't the same for all the programs. When using a cache program, the most time is saved with ARJ. ARJ accesses the hard drive much more frequently than the other compression programs. That's why you get better results when you combine it with a cache program.

PKZIP doesn't benefit very much, because it's already fast without the cache. ZOO also benefits from using a cache program. However, since cache programs don't influence compression ratios, ZOO is still at the bottom of the scale.

Data Compression Elements

2

Data Compression Command Line Structure

One reason why users don't fully use the capabilities of compression programs is because of the complicated syntax. (Syntax refers to the form in which commands are entered.)

The following command line is a good example of this awkward syntax:

We discussed data compression theory in Chapter 1. In this chapter, we'll discuss data compression programs in detail. At first, it may seem like compression programs are easy to use. However, it's difficult to use the advanced features of these programs. Compression programs usually include instructions in a text file. However, these files confuse users because they don't provide enough information about the commands and switches. So, even after reading the instructions, you still may not understand the options included with the program.

So, unfortunately most users don't understand how to use compression programs and what the terminology means. In this chapter, we'll explain the technical aspects of compression programs.

```
LHA <command> [/option[-+012|WDIR]] <archive[.LZH]> [DIR\] [filenames]
```

As you can see, it may be difficult to understand this command line. However, once you become more familiar with these command lines, you'll be able to ignore the brackets and slashes. Then you can concentrate on the essentials and discover that compression programs have similar structures.

The structure of a command isn't quite as clear as the example shown in the following figure. However, this is what constitutes inputting a command. Only four components (not including the names of the compression programs) make up the command line of a compression program. Some of these components aren't needed to run the program.

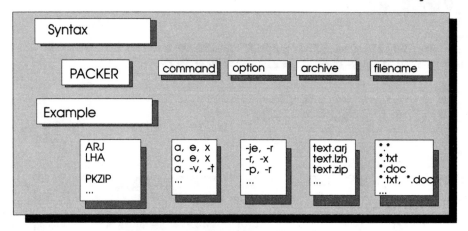

Structure of a command line for data compression

If you want to get the most out of your compression program, use the powerful options that the program includes. With some patience and experience, you'll be able to do this easily.

Data compression components

The following table summarizes the data compression components.

Command (Required)	When you type the command, you're specifying the kind of task the compressor is supposed to perform. For example, simple commands, such as Add or Update, are frequently used, while commands such as Delete or Rename aren't used as often.
Switch (Optional)	Use switches to control the execution of the command and specify deviations from the standard procedure. For example, you would add a switch to the command to specify that subdirectories should be included when you compress a directory. In this book, we use the terms option, switch, and parameter interchangeably, depending on the specific program.
Archive name (Required)	The archive name must appear in the command. Usually specifying the file extension (e.g., ARC, ZIP, etc.) isn't necessary because the compression program assigns the extension automatically.
Files (Optional)	At the end of the command line, specify the files you want processed. You can specify names and wildcards (?, *) with most data compression programs. Depending on the command being processed, the filename you select refers to files in the archive or on the drive. If you don't specify a filename, the program assumes it should process all files (*.*).

The following table contains example command lines for various compression programs:

Packer	Command	Switch	Archive	Files
ARJ	l		TEST	
ARJ	u	-WC:\	TEST	*.TXT *.DOC
LHA	a	-r-x	ARCHIVE	*.*
PKZIP	-a	-r	TABLE	*.XL?
PAK	a	/Gxyz	SECRET	Packer

If the command line structure is still confusing to you, access the help functions. To do this, use the switch "/?" to display information about the most important commands.

```
PKZIP  Enter
ARJ  Enter        (simple overview)
ARJ /?      Enter     (complete overview)
LHA  Enter
```

Each compression program provides a different amount of commands and switches. For example, PKZIP provides numerous switches. If you start the help functions, you'll see four screens containing various combinations of commands and switches. All these functions and switches are part of the respective program.

There are also different options for controlling program functions. For example, some compressors differentiate between the packing module and the unpacking module. PKZIP and its counterpart PKUNZIP make this distinction. Other independent program modules analyze archives or convert archives into self-extracting archives.

Archive Files

The file extensions ZIP, LHA, LZH, ARC, and ARJ identify archive files. Whenever you compress or decompress data, you'll meet with archives. An archive is simply the PC version of a physical archive (i.e., a place where important documents are stored).

Files are packed into a separate area when they're compressed. They cannot be processed until you retrieve them again with a data decompression program.

Structure of archives

By storing information with each archived file, the compression program is able to locate archives. There is also different information for the archive itself. Let's look at the schematic structure of a typical PC archive:

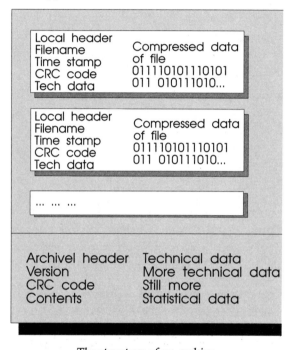

The structure of an archive

Every archive is a network that consists of the following:

❖ Data from each archived file

❖ Local data

❖ Information about the total archive

The local data (i.e., the data that belongs to the individually archived files) is divided into the local header and the compressed data. The header contains important information that is needed for decompressing the file. It's impossible to decompress the file without this information. It would even be conceivable to manage all the statistical data in one place, along with the header data of the central header. However, this would be dangerous.

If an error occurs somewhere in an archive, most likely the entire archive isn't useless. Since the archive is divided into individual archived files, the damage is usually limited to only the file containing the error.

Every archive also has a global header, sometimes called an archive header. This global header contains statistical data that isn't important to the individual files. However, this statistical data is crucial to the total structure of the archive.

The following is a short section from the header information of a PKZIP archive. It will give you an idea of the complexity of data compression:

❖ Central header signature

❖ Packer version

❖ Required version for unpacking

❖ General information

❖ Date of last change

❖ Time of last change

❖ 32 bit CRC code

❖ Compressed size and normal size

Remember, this is only a small section. The entire list of information is much larger. If you add the local headers, you'll understand why the pure compression ratios are drastically different from the final size. This is especially true for smaller files.

The local headers make it possible to make changes to archives. All the important information about the individual files is stored in the headers. To update the files in the archive, simply compare the local header. You can find it quickly in the archive. You can also change the names of archived files just as quickly. To do this, simply make a minor change to the header.

Determine the contents of an archive quickly by having the data compression program go from header to header and collect the statistical data stored in each one.

Self-extracting Archives

Sometimes it's difficult to unpack archives if a new version of the compression program is being used. Because of this problem, developers created self-extracting archives. With these archives, a small program is added to the archive that handles unpacking. This turns a passive archive into an active program that unpacks itself on demand.

A self-extracting archive has two advantages:

1. The data compression program to access the compressed data is no longer needed.

2. Beginners can access compressed data, even if they've never seen a data compression program or the complicated commands.

So, instead of typing

```
PKUNZIP TRANSFER
```

you only need to type

```
TRANSFER
```

Structure of an SFX archive

The term "self-extracting archive" is abbreviated as an "SFX" archive. The only difference in the structure of a normal archive and an SFX archive is that an SFX archive contains additional bytes. These bytes are the commands of the program that automatically unpack the archived files.

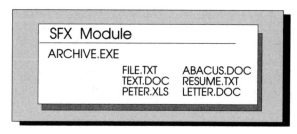

Structure of an SFX archive

The above figure shows a decompression module that is added to the archive. The archive is no longer named ARCHIVE.ZIP or .ARJ or .LZH but ARCHIVE.EXE because the archive now includes a program for decompressing the archived files.

The size of this module varies, depending on the compressor. The module could be 1,000 bytes or, in an ARJ archive, it could be more than 15K. Obviously, this is a lot to send through a modem. The varying sizes of the module are based on its capacity. ARJ provides numerous commands that you can use with the archive without ARJ. Other SFX modules are only able to decompress.

When you're working with a data compression program, you can handle SFX archives like normal archives. For example, the same command is used to delete all the TXT files in the TRANS archive of a normal archive or of an SFX archive. For a normal archive, enter the following

```
PKZIP -d TRANS *.TXT
```

and for an SFX archive, enter:

```
PKZIP -d TRANS.EXE *.TXT
```

EXE Compression Programs

The files located in archives must be decompressed before you can access them. Although this procedure is also necessary for SFX archives, it's faster and more efficient than that used for normal archive files.

The program developed by Fabrice Bellard was the first to approach this problem from a different perspective. His idea was to archive programs so they could be decompressed and executed in RAM.

Making programs smaller

You can use this method to reduce programs without limiting their functions. This method reduces the local requirements to about half the original program size. Since you no longer need to decompress the programs before running them, this is an effective gain of disk space.

Unfortunately, there are disadvantages to this method. What you gain in disk space, you lose in time. You cannot immediately load and run compressed programs when you start the PC. Instead, you must decompress them first. This procedure requires a certain amount of time. The slower your hard drive and PC, the more you'll notice how long this takes. However, if you have a 386 or faster PC, you shouldn't really notice a decrease in speed.

This method of compression doesn't solve all disk space problems. You cannot make some programs smaller (for example, Windows programs). Larger DOS programs that work with overlay files (program segments called into memory when needed) can also cause problems. Older COM programs can also be difficult. However, COM programs are smaller than EXE programs, so normally you won't have to worry about compressing them.

Decompressing Data

3

Integrated or diversified

Not all data compression programs use the same procedure for decompressing files. Some programs handle both compressing and decompressing. The functions are then started by using command switches. For example, the following command compresses files using LHARC:

```
LHA a CONSTITU
```

The files of the archive are decompressed with the following command:

```
LHA e CONSTITU
```

An archive must eventually be restored to its original state. Usually this procedure isn't difficult. However, since compression programs are so complex, you may come across some problems.

In this chapter we'll discuss the different aspects of decompression. Besides the general operations, we'll discuss the characteristics of the individual compression programs in detail.

If you already have complete compressed archives, you can continue immediately. Otherwise, first you should familiarize yourself with compressing files and creating archives. Refer to Chapter 4 for this information.

Note that a single letter determines which function is started.

Some programs can only perform one function. For example, the PKZIP/PKUNZIP pair is primarily responsible for packing and unpacking ZIP archives, respectively. However, both PKZIP and PKUNZIP include functions for managing files in the archive and providing important information. Therefore, it's possible to delegate all elementary functions to external programs. Several programs deal exclusively with manipulating and processing archives.

For example, these programs can do the following (among others):

❖ List

❖ Delete

❖ Repair

❖ Convert

Such programs are used at the DOS level along with the specified archives. In the case of PKZIP, the command to compress would be the following:

```
PKZIP -a CONSTITU
```

You would have to use the PKUNZIP program to decompress the archive:

```
PKUNZIP CONSTITU
```

In this case, a command letter isn't needed because PKUNZIP's only purpose is to decompress archives. However, PKUNZIP also contains commands and parameters that make decompressing files more flexible and efficient. We'll talk more about these options later.

Decompressing Archives

The process for opening archives and removing files is usually very simple. Transferring all or only specific files from an archive to a directory requires only a few parameters. Since you can remove files individually or in groups, you don't have to extract all the files from the archive and then delete unneeded files on the DOS level using the DEL command.

With all the compression programs, files with the same name can be overwritten by compressed data. However, if you don't want this to happen, you can use the additional parameters described below. The decompression command is always used the same way:

1. PKUNZIP CONSTITU *.TXT *.DOC *.WRI

2. LHA e CONSTITU

3. ARJ e CONSTITU !TEXTS -x*.BAK

The above examples demonstrate how easy it is to decompress archives. If you look ahead to Chapter 4, you'll see how these commands work.

1. PKUNZIP extracts from the CONSTITU archive only files with the .TXT, .DOC or .WRI extension.

2. LHA decompresses all files contained in the CONSTITU archive.

3. ARJ removes all files from the CONSTITU archive that appear in the TEXTS list file. Only files with the .BAK extension are not removed.

Program	Command Line	Program	Command Line
LHA	LHA e CONSTITU	ARJ	ARJ e CONSTITU
ICE	ICE e CONSTITU	ZOO	ZOO -extract CONSTITU ZOO e/x CONSTITU
PKZIP	PKUNZIP CONSTITU	PAK	PAK e CONSTITU
PKPAK	PKUNPAK CONSTITU		

Without additional file specifications, the data compression program automatically assumes that all the files contained in the archive should be decompressed into the current directory. However, you can specify an individual file or several files.

The following examples: decompress all the files in an archive named ARC whose file extensions begin with "DB" or "XL."

```
ARJ e ARC *.DB? *.XL?

PKUNPAK ARC *.DB? *.XL?

LHA e ARC *.DB? *.XL?

PAK e ARC *.DB? *.XL?
```

Besides simply listing filenames, some compression programs also process list files. The filenames, which can then be evaluated by the program, are saved in such files. PKUNZIP and ARJ can process these lists. Simply add the filename to the command line:

```
PKUNZIP ARC *.DB? *.XL? @TEXTS

ARJ e ARC *.DB? *.XL? !TEXTS
```

In the above examples, the direct file entries will return all files in the TEXTS list file. Remember that PKUNZIP and ARJ use different symbols to indicate list files. With PKUNZIP, you must use an "at" symbol (@) and with ARJ, you must place an exclamation point (!) in front of the list. These symbols are needed to notify the program that it must evaluate the "TEXTS" file contents instead of processing the name of the list file itself.

ARJ is the only compression program that lets you exclude certain files during decompression. As with compression, it's possible to name a file more than once and combine them with list files by using the "-x" option.

```
ARJ e ARC -x*.BAK -x*.COM -x!NOTT.HAT
```

This command extracts all files from the ARC archive except files with the .COM or .EXE extensions and the files named in the NOTT.HAT list.

As you know, PKZIP also lets you exclude files from compression. However, for decompressing data, you must use PKUNZIP, which doesn't provide this feature.

Selecting working directories

If you don't want to place the decompressed data in the current directory, you can send the files to any directory on any storage medium. To do this, simply enter the target path of your files after the archive name, such as

```
LHA e ARC C:\EXAMPLE\ *.TXT *.DB? *.XL?
```

or

```
ARJ e ARC C:\EXAMPLE\ *.TXT *.DB? *.XL?
```

As you can see, a trailing backslash (\) is added to the "C:\EXAMPLE" directory entry. If this backslash was used with the DOS command, an error would occur. However, with compression programs, this backslash is needed for the operation to run.

Enter the directory as follows:

```
PKUNZIP ARC C:\EXAMPLE\ *.TXT
PKUNPAK ARC C:\EXAMPLE\ *.TXT
LHA e ARC C:\EXAMPLE\ *.TXT
```

```
ICE e ARC C:\EXAMPLE\ *.TXT
ARJ e ARC C:\EXAMPLE(\) *.TXT
PAK e ARC C:\EXAMPLE\*.TXT
```

Remember, the file extension (here *.TXT) must be entered directly after the target path only with PAK. This procedure resembles that of DOS commands (for example, COPY C:\EXAMPLE*.TXT). However, the target directory must already exist.

Creating directories

All the data compression programs listed in the table (except PAK) let you create directories. If a directory doesn't exist, it can be created.

In the following command line, ARJ quickly determines that "C:\WORD\EXAMPLE" doesn't exist. In this case, the program prompts for your permission to create this directory.

```
ARJ e ARC C:\WORD\EXAMPLE\
```

If you confirm this action, the directory is automatically created. Any additional files will be decompressed into the new directory. If choose not to create the directory, ARJ tries to decompress the files at the designated place, but won't be able to because the target directory doesn't exist. In this case, you must enter a new name for each file or another path.

```
C:\EXAMPLE>arj e arc c:\winword\doc\
ARJ 2.41a Copyright (c) 1990-93 Robert K Jung. Jul 10 1993
*** This SHAREWARE program is NOT REGISTERED for use in a business, commercial,
*** government, or institutional environment except for evaluation purposes.

Processing archive: ARC.ARJ
Archive created: 1996-01-03 11:38:42, modified: 1996-01-03 11:38:42
C:\WINWORD\DOC\CHAP07.DOC, Create this directory? y
Extracting CHAP07.DOC    to C:\WINWORD\DOC\CHAP07.DOC    OK
Extracting CHAP05.DOC    to C:\WINWORD\DOC\CHAP05.DOC    OK
Extracting UPGRADFX.DOC  to C:\WINWORD\DOC\UPGRADFX.DOC  OK
Extracting CHAP04.DOC    to C:\WINWORD\DOC\CHAP04.DOC    OK
Extracting CHAP03.DOC    to C:\WINWORD\DOC\CHAP03.DOC    OK
Extracting CHAP01.DOC    to C:\WINWORD\DOC\CHAP01.DOC    OK
Extracting CHAP02.DOC    to C:\WINWORD\DOC\CHAP02.DOC    OK
Extracting CHAP04A.DOC   to C:\WINWORD\DOC\CHAP04A.DOC   OK
Extracting CHAP03A.DOC   to C:\WINWORD\DOC\CHAP03A.DOC   OK
Extracting CHAP02A.DOC   to C:\WINWORD\DOC\CHAP02A.DOC   OK
    10 file(s)

C:\EXAMPLE>
```

A directory is created

> ARJ only creates directories if the target path ends with a backslash. So, if you're sure that the target directory already exists, you don't have to enter the backslash.

LHA and ICE operate basically the same way. Needed directories are created automatically. If you specify that a directory should be created, any additional files will be decompressed immediately. If you choose not to create the new directory, you'll be asked to confirm the compression of each file individually. However, the option of entering the name of the file individually, as in the case of ARJ, doesn't exist.

In the case of PKUNZIP and PKUNPAK, it's important that the directories already exist. Otherwise, an error will occur.

With PKUNZIP, this behavior can be changed with the "-d" option. If this option is included in the command, the required directories are created automatically. Therefore, the backslash (\) isn't needed.

```
PKUNZIP -d ARC C:\EXAMPLE *.TXT
```

LHA lets you decompress archives directly into several directories simultaneously. This feature is particularly helpful when you've archived many files of different types and then want to work on them separately. Specify this in the command line by entering more than one directory. All the filenames following the name of a directory will be placed in this working directory.

```
LHA e EXAMPLES C:\DATA\WINWORD\*.BAK C:\DATA\WINWORD\EXTRA\*.DOC
```

```
C:\>LHA E EXAMPLES C:\DATA\WINWORD\ *.BAK C:\DATA\WINWORD\EXTRA\ *.DOC

Extracting from archive : EXAMPLES.LZH

'C:/DATA/WINWORD/CHAP03.BAK' : Make directory? [Y/N] Y
Melted    CHAP03.BAK    oooooooo
Melted    CHAP07.BAK    oooooooo
'C:/DATA/WINWORD/EXTRA/CHAP07.DOC' : Make directory? [Y/N] Y
Melted    CHAP07.DOC    oooooo
Melted    CHAP05.DOC    ooooooooo
Melted    CHAP04.DOC    oooooooo
Melted    CHAP03.DOC    ooooooooo
Melted    CHAP01.DOC    oooooo
Melted    CHAP02.DOC    ooooo

C:\>
```

Separate working directory in LHA and ICE

The italicized options are the working directories. All files with the .DOC extension are compressed into the C:\WORD directory, and all XL- and DB-files are compressed into the C:\DATA directory. If these directories don't exist yet, they are created by LHA after prompting you for confirmation. So, conflicts are no longer possible. If a file was already decompressed into a working directory, it cannot be decompressed again into a different directory. Although it isn't possible with this procedure, duplicating files could be helpful:

```
LHA e REPORTS C:\TO_ME\ *.DOC *.DB? C:\TO_YOU\ *.DOC
```

PAK includes this feature in a similar format. By the entry of several files you can control where certain files will be decompressed. For example, the following command

```
PAK e ARC C:\WORD\*.DOC C:\DATA\*.DB? C:\DATA\*.XL?
```

decompresses the following types of files:

File	Directory
DOC	Into the C:\WORD directory
XL?	Into the C:\DATA directory
DB?	Into the C:\DATA directory

PAK isn't as flexible as LHA, because if several file types must be decompressed into a directory, you must then enter a separate target path for each in the command line. If the target path is unavailable, PAK will skip decompressing the file ("xxx" skipped).

Preventing prompts

The prompt asking whether a directory, which doesn't exist, should be created during decompression can be suppressed. To do this in LHA, ICE, and ARJ, use the parameters in the table to the right.

Option	Command
-m	LHA e -m ARC C:\REPORT\ ICE e -m ARC C:\REPORT\
-y	ARJ e -y ARC C:\REPORT\

Not all data compression programs can easily redirect the output of the extracted file into a different directory (or drive). However, you can use the DOS command CD to jump into the target directory before you begin decompressing. Then you can start the decompression process. In this way, the files will still be placed into the desired directory.

```
C:
CD \WORD\REPORTS
ZOO e ARC
```

Protecting existing files

When you decompress archives, sometimes files with the same name already exist in the current or working directory. Unlike the DOS commands COPY and XCOPY, the compression programs don't immediately overwrite the file in the target directory with the uncompressed version. Instead, the data compression program notice whether files have the same names. It then responds as follows:

❖ Skip the file.

❖ Indicate that a file of the same name already exists and asks whether the file should be overwritten.

❖ Compare the ages of the files and overwrite the file in the target directory, if it is older.

❖ Let you specify another name for the uncompressed file or do this automatically.

The following figure shows how ARJ responds to this situation:

```
C:\WINWORD\DOC>arj x arc
ARJ 2.41a Copyright (c) 1990-93 Robert K Jung. Jul 10 1993
*** This SHAREWARE program is NOT REGISTERED for use in a business, commercial
*** government, or institutional environment except for evaluation purposes.

Processing archive: ARC.ARJ
Archive created: 1996-01-03 11:38:42, modified: 1996-01-03 11:38:42
Extracting CHAP07.DOC      OK
Extracting CHAP05.DOC      OK
ARJ      6656  95-12-20 11:42:24, DISK      6656  95-12-20 11:42:24
UPGRADFX.DOC  is same or newer, Overwrite? y
Extracting UPGRADFX.DOC    OK
Extracting CHAP04.DOC      OK
Extracting CHAP03.DOC      OK
Extracting CHAP01.DOC      OK
Extracting CHAP02.DOC      OK
Extracting CHAP04A.DOC     OK
Extracting CHAP03A.DOC     OK
Extracting CHAP02A.DOC     OK
    10 file(s)

C:\WINWORD\DOC>
```

ARJ finds files with the same names

40

ARJ interrupts the procedure and prompts what action you want to take. The following table shows the four possible actions:

Letter	Effect
Y (yes)	ARJ decompresses the file in question and overwrites the version already on the disk.
N (no)	The file is decompressed, but you can enter a new name for the archived file. The file will be skipped if you press .
A (all)	All remaining files are decompressed without additional prompts. Existing files with the same name are overwritten.
Q (quit)	The decompression procedure stops and the file is not overwritten.

The other data compression programs provide similar options. However, you usually only have choice between Yes or No.

Decompressing Archives And Safety Prompts

Occasionally, you should suppress the compression program's safety prompts and answer all the prompts at once with "Y" ("Yes"). By doing this, the compression procedure won't be interrupted by prompts that you must answer. You should suppress the safety prompts when you want to decompress batch files quickly.

The tables in the following section specify which options should be used to switch off certain safety prompts in the different compression programs.

PKUNZIP and safety prompts

Without additional options, PKUNZIP always displays a prompt when there are similar files in the working directory. The difference between -f and -n is the following:

-n   files which are not yet present in the target directory are also decompressed.

-o   overwrites all files, regardless of age.

The following command decompresses all .TXT files from the ARC archive. Any files in the target directory that have the same name are replaced; safety prompts aren't displayed.

```
PKUNZIP -o ARC *.TXT
```

Only files present in both the target directory and the archive are decompressed with the following command. Safety prompts won't appear if the decompressed files are more current.

```
PKUNZIP -f ARC
```

ARJ and safety prompts

ARJ displays the safety prompt if a file with the same name already exists. The file's age doesn't matter. Therefore, it's dangerous to switch off all prompts. However, by using special options, you can control how the age of files is handled by ARJ.

Option	Function
e	Standard command for decompressing.
-n	New. Decompresses files only if a file with the same name doesn't exist.
-f	Freshen. Decompresses files only if an older version exists in the directory.
-u	Update. Decompresses files only if a file with the same name doesn't exist on the target directory or such a file is older. It combines -n and -f.
-jo	Creates a new name for the archived file when a file with the same name exists.
-y	General 'Yes' to all questions.

Qualified "Yes"

-jy..	Option beginning for qualified YES.
..c	Prompt during creation of a new directory.
..d	Prompt on deleting a file from a directory.
..n	Prompt after a new filename.
..o	Prompt relative to overwriting an existing file.

The "-y" switch is the simplest YES you can specify in ARJ. It's also the most comprehensive YES, because almost every prompt is suppressed. So, the prompts can be switched off as needed. The introduction of "restricted prompts" is accomplished with the "-jy" switch. You can then attach one or more additional letters to these two, depending on which prompts you want to suppress.

```
ARJ e -jyco ARC C:\WORD\REPORT\
```

The above command prevents prompts from appearing when a new directory is created or when existing files are overwritten. However, instead of deciding whether the current or the archived file contains the more important information, you can have ARJ save both files together.

With "-jo", you tell ARJ to create a new name in the case of a duplicate name for the decompressed files. ARJ simply deletes the file extension and replaces it with a number. For example:

```
LETTER.TXT    —>    LETTER.000
```

Now you must identify the new file and change the name again.

ARJ renames files

LHA and ICE and safety prompts

By default during compression, LHA and ICE do not overwrite files if a newer file with the same name is found in the target directory. Older files are overwritten following the usual prompt. Use the following options to change this procedure:

Option	Function
e	Standard command for decompressing archives.
-c	The file date of the archived file is ignored. Therefore, even recent files can be overwritten.
-m	Prevents the safety prompts from being displayed.
-m2	Only for LHA. Decompresses files with the same name, but generates new file extensions in numerical format (for example, LETTER.000).

```
LHA e -c ARC *.TXT
```

By using the above command, LHA decompresses all .TXT files in the archive into the current directory. By using the -c option, each file having the same name is overwritten following a prompt, regardless of its date. The same result is produced with the following command:

```
ICE e -cm *.TXT   (or ICE e -c -m *.TXT )
```

However, files with the same name are deleted without the prompt. If you use the following command:

```
LHA e -cm2 *.TXT  ( or LHA e -c -m2 *.TXT )
```

files with the same name aren't overwritten. Instead, the decompressed files receive new names, which are clearly distinguished from the versions in the target directory. "LETTER.TXT" then becomes "LETTER.000" (or another number, depending on which are available).

ICE files can be decompressed by LHA. Also, ICE may be able to decompress LHA files (depending on the age of the programs).

Since LHA is a program descendent of ICE, LHA knows all the compression and decompression algorithms of ICE. However, ICE doesn't know the more recent methods. Therefore, LHA files that were compressed with the current compression method cannot be processed.

44

```
LHA e ARC.ICE
```

or

```
ICE e *.LZH
```

PAK and safety prompts

Option		Function
e		Decompression command.
/WP	*Write Over- Prompt*	Displays a safety prompt, if a file already exists (default setting).
/WN	*Write Over Never*	Existing files are never overwritten.
/WA	*Write Over Always*	Existing files are overwritten without prompts.
/WO	*Write Over Older*	Existing files are overwritten only if they are older than the version in the archive.
/D		Decompresses only those files from the archive which also exist in the target directory. Can be combined with all /Wx parameters.

If you've defined more than one /W option in a command, the safer option will take priority over the less safe. This means that the option that overwrites the least number of files is the option that will be used. Therefore, /WN has higher priority than /WP, which has higher priority than /WO and /WA.

```
PAK e /WN ARC
```

With the above command, all files from the ARC archive are decompressed into the current directory. If any files in the archive have the same name, they won't be decompressed.

```
PAK e /D /WO ARC C:\TEXTS\*.TXT C:\DAT\*.DB?
```

The above command specifies that files in the ARC archive that have the .TXT file extension will be decompressed into the C:\TEXTS directory and the .DB? files will be decompressed into the C:\DAT directory. Obviously, only the files that appear in the archive and target directory (/D) are included in the selection process. Only relatively old files are replaced by more current ones (/WO).

ZOO and safety prompts

Option		Function
e,x		Alternative decompression commands.
S	*(Supercede)*	Existing files are overwritten in the target directory, even if they are more recent than the archived versions.
O	*(Overwrite)*	The safety prompt doesn't appear.
N	*(Neverlands)*	The archive is being tested. The files are being decompressed into an empty space.

ZOO normally (when there are no special parameters) overwrites all older files in the target directory, after the safety prompt appears. If you use the O option with S, archived and obsolete files may overwrite current and important information.

Be sure to use uppercase O.

```
ZOO eO ARC
```

With the above command, ZOO unpacks the ARC archive into the current directory (e) and overwrites older files without safety prompts (O).

```
ZOO eSO ARC
```

With this command, all the files of the current directory will be overwritten by archived files that have the same name, regardless of the age of the file (S). A safety prompt doesn't appear (O).

PKUNPAK and safety prompts

Option		Function
-f	*(freshen)*	Only files, which are older than the archived files, located in the target directory are decompressed. Safety prompts don't appear.
-n	*(newer)*	Newer archived files overwrite existing files. A safety prompt doesn't appear.
-o	*(overwrite)*	Existing files are overwritten without additional safety prompts.
-d	*(directory)*	Creates necessary directories automatically.

46

PKUNPAK's decompression process is the same as PKUNZIP's process. However, remember that the Freshen option "-f" isn't available in PAK.

```
PKUNPAK -r ARC *.D*
```

The above command decompresses all files which have extensions beginning with "D", from the ARC archive. If files with the same name are located in the target directory, they are deleted, regardless of their age. Safety prompts aren't displayed.

```
PKUNZIP -n ARC C:\TRANSFER\
```

With the above command, all files are decompressed from the archive into C:\TRANSFER. If a file with the same name already exists, this file is overwritten, if it's older. Safety prompts don't appear.

Decompressing Directories

Now that you've learned how to decompress individual files, we'll discuss decompressing entire directories. We've divided these topics into two separate sections because only a few compression programs, such as PKZIP LHA, ICE, and ARJ, can automatically compress entire directory trees.

You can decompress an archive with or without the directory and path information. The second method (without path information) works like the normal decompression of archives. This means that it doesn't disturb directory information. In this case, "e" is used as a command switch, and the files are decompressed together into a directory.

The directory structure is restored in the target directory by decompressing an archive with path information. So, it's possible to archive and move entire directory trees easily. Use "x" as the command letter for this decompression method.

All the options for the "normal" decompression of files that we've discussed also apply to decompressing directory archives. Therefore, in this section, we'll concentrate on the problems that can occur with archived directories.

Before you can decompress archives with directories, obviously first the archives must be compressed properly. With ARJ, you don't have to worry about correct compression, because path information is incorporated into the archive automatically. LHA and ICE, however, usually store only the filenames. Therefore, these programs need a special command to include the pathnames when the files are compressed. This also applies to PKZIP. (For more information on using the different compression programs, see Chapter 4.)

It's easy to decompress archives that have compressed directory structures. Although many parameters were needed for each command during the compression process, the data compression program can (almost) automatically restore the directories in an archive. If the directory tree was originally stored properly, with most compression programs, you can simply enter the correct start command. For example, with PKUNZIP, enter the following:

```
PKUNZIP -d TRANS A:\
```

In this case, an archive, including all files and directories, will be transferred to the diskette. Simply confirm the prompts that appear, if an existing file may be overwritten or a new directory should be created. (As we explained in the previous section, you can switch off these prompts.)

Relative and absolute paths

To understand how directory structures are stored in archives, you must understand the concept of relative and absolute directory positions. We'll explain these concepts by using an example.

Suppose a person rings your doorbell and asks you the quickest way to get to the bus station. You tell this person to go the second traffic light and turn left. The bus station is about 2 miles down, on the right side of the street.

Perhaps this is the quickest way to the bus station from your house. However, these directions are correct only from your current location. If the person had stopped and asked your neighbor on the next street for directions, he/she would have gotten a different answer. So, the directions you've given are valid only from your location at the moment (i.e., they are correct "relative" to your position). This is similar to a relative path.

You could also answer this person's question another way. Instead of using your house as a starting point, you can use a stationary and specific location. Therefore, you could change your directions to "stand with your back to the water tower, go down the street to the fourth traffic signal, turn right, and then left."

Unlike the first description, this way (or path) is based on a fixed location. The starting point of the path (the water tower) is absolute and always the same. In this case, it doesn't matter whether you give these directions while standing on your front porch or from your favorite restaurant.

To apply this example to relative and absolute paths, replace the stationary water tower with the root directory on the hard drive. Regardless of the size of your directory structure, the root directory is unique and can be reached from any location. Therefore, all path descriptions starting from this point reach their goal (if the path is specified correctly).

Restoring directory structures

Restoring directory structures is closely related to compressing data. The following figure of a tree structure should help you understand the examples we'll present in the following sections. In this directory structure (which isn't the only one on drive C:), there are various files which must be archived according to their purpose.

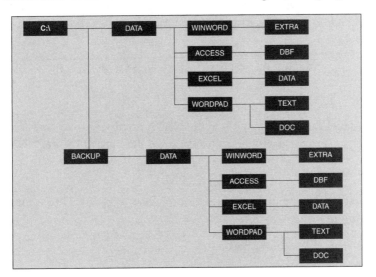

An example of a typical directory tree

If the archive was compressed properly, it should be easy to decompress the files. Use the following commands to retrieve both files and directories:

```
PKUNZIP -d DATA C:\DATA\WINWORD
ARJ x -y DATA C:\DATA\WINWORD
ICE x -x DATA C:\DATA\WINWORD
LHA x DATA C:\DATA\WINWORD
```

As you can see, the commands of the individual programs differ only slightly. With all the compression programs, you can decompress the archive wherever you want by specifying a target directory.

In the following sections, you'll learn how to prepare the archive for later compression and which parameters are important for "directory-bound" archives.

PKUNZIP and restoring directory structures

PKUNZIP needs the -d option to create directories automatically. Without this option, all archived files will be written to the target directory without path information. As a result, the files, which were still separated by a directory in the archive, are now grouped together in the target directory. If there are files with the same names, they won't be decompressed.

Since absolute paths of files aren't saved by PKZIP, they cannot be decompressed by PKUNZIP. Whether the entire directory structure is transferred correctly depends on you.

For example, to archive the BACKUP directory completely, use the PKZIP command:

```
PKZIP -a -rP DATA \BACKUP\*.*
```

The P switch saves the complete path in the DATA archive. Now you must decompress the archive at the proper location. To do this, use the path entry in PKUNZIP.

```
PKUNZIP -d DATA A:\
```

The above command completely restores the archive on diskette. The required directories are created automatically.

```
PKUNZIP -d DATA C:\COPIES\ *.BAK
```

With the above command, all files with the .BAK extension are decompressed under the C:\COPIES directory. Any directory containing a .BAK file is created automatically. The new directory structure will appear as follows:

```
C:\data>CD..

C:\>PKUNZIP -D DATA

PKUNZIP (R)    FAST!    Extract Utility    Version 2.04g  02-01-93
Copr. 1989-1993 PKWARE Inc. All Rights Reserved. Shareware Version
PKUNZIP Reg. U.S. Pat. and Tm. Off.

■ 80486 CPU detected.
■ XMS version 3.00 detected.
■ DPMI version 0.90 detected.

Searching ZIP: DATA.ZIP
   Inflating: DATA/WINWORD/CHAP07.DOC
   Inflating: DATA/WINWORD/CHAP05.DOC
   Inflating: DATA/WINWORD/UPGRADFX.DOC
   Inflating: DATA/WINWORD/CHAP04.DOC
   Inflating: DATA/WINWORD/CHAP03.DOC
   Inflating: DATA/WINWORD/CHAP01.DOC
   Inflating: DATA/WINWORD/CHAP02.DOC
   Inflating: DATA/WINWORD/CHAP04A.DOC
   Inflating: DATA/WINWORD/CHAP03A.DOC
   Inflating: DATA/WINWORD/CHAP02A.DOC

C:\>
```

Decompressed archive with directories

In the following command:

```
PKUNZIP DATA C:\BACKUP\
```

PKUNZIP decompresses all files in DATA into the C:\BACKUP directory, if it exists. Because the "-d" parameter wasn't included, C:\BACKUP and the directories contained in the archive won't be created.

LHA and ICE and restoring directory structures

Unlike PKZIP, LHA and ICE save the paths as they were defined in the command line during compression. So, the following command line is possible:

```
LHA a -rx DATA C:\DATA\WINWORD\*.*
```

This command always works correctly because it includes the absolute path to the data that must be compressed. To confirm this, use the "v" command:

```
C:\>LHA V DATA

Listing of archive : DATA.LZH

  Name           Original    Packed  Ratio   Date      Time    Attr Type  CRC
-------------- ---------- -------- ------ -------- -------- ---- ----- ----
/DATA/WINWORD/CHAP07.DOC
                   65536     21643   33.0% 95-12-28 21:05:12 a--w -lh5- 59DE
/DATA/WINWORD/CHAP05.DOC
                   69120     23423   33.9% 95-12-28 21:05:12 a--w -lh5- 6EA7
/DATA/WINWORD/CHAP04.DOC
                   59392     19918   33.5% 95-12-14 15:38:00 a--w -lh5- FEF5
/DATA/WINWORD/CHAP03.DOC
                   72192     23804   33.0% 95-12-14 16:29:32 a--w -lh5- F121
/DATA/WINWORD/CHAP01.DOC
                   44544     15657   35.1% 95-12-14 14:46:06 a--w -lh5- 65ED
/DATA/WINWORD/CHAP02.DOC
                   38400     12323   32.1% 95-12-15 09:38:18 a--w -lh5- 2791
-------------- ---------- -------- ------ -------- -------- 
   6 files        349184    116768  33.4% 96-01-03 14:13:16

C:\>
```

Archive with absolute path data

Unfortunately, you may encounter problems when decompressing this LHA archive, because the files cannot be decompressed into any directory other than the main directory. The absolute path entries (the leading backslash makes that clear) will always begin in a \BACKUP directory when restored.

If you want to be able to decompress the archive into any directory, you should use a different compression procedure. Avoid including absolute paths in the command line. To do this, use two commands instead of one:

```
CD \
LHA a -rx XB BVB\*.*          '
```

The same files will be compressed. Only the leading backslash in the command line is missing. However, to ensure that the files will be found, the preceding jump to the main directory is important. Now you can decompress the archive into any directory:

```
LHA x VB C:\COPIES\
```

If any directories don't exist on the target drive, they are created automatically by LHA. The "x" command has a built-in confirmation that answers the prompt. If you want to confirm the prompt yourself, add the "-m" option:

```
LHA x -m VB C:\COPIES\
```

ICE works in almost the same way as LHARC. However, there are a few small differences. The version of ICE we're using (Version 1.14 of 7/15/89) is slightly older than LHARC. Most of these differences involve compression. However, it is important whether the "-r" parameter, for recursive collection, and "-x", for switch on expanded filenames (path information), are switched. In ICE, the correct sequence is:

```
ICE a -xr ...
```

If these options are set up differently, they won't make any sense. In this case, ICE will stop working and display an error message about finding duplicate filenames.

ARJ and restoring directory structures

ARJ again provides the longest list of options, even if they aren't needed for the decompression. Obviously, the structure of the directory tree is already established in the archive. So, you can immediately begin decompressing the data. Since the directory operations are being used, the command letter "x" is now used instead of "e":

```
ARJ x DATA C:\COPIES
```

If additional options aren't specified, ARJ always saves and compresses the files relatively. Therefore, it's possible to transfer an archived directory tree to any desired location. In the above example, the familiar BACKUP tree will always fall under the C:\COPIES directory. Remember that with ARJ, even empty directories are again decompressed or created, if you collected them with the "-a1" option during compression.

```
ARJ a -r -a1 DATA C:\BACKUP\*.*
```

The safety prompts, which have appeared several times, can be suppressed. For information on how to do this, refer the first section in this chapter. You can also enter a comprehensive "YES":

```
ARJ x -y DATA
```

The "-y" option ensures that the decompression process won't be interrupted by prompts indicating missing directories or duplicate filenames.

You can force ARJ to decompress the archive into the main directory. Simply attach the "-jf" option to the command:

```
ARJ a -r DATA A:\*.*
```

ARJ archives all files and the entire directory structure on the diskette in drive A. If this structure should be transferred to drive C, use "-jf" to force the data compression program to decompress the archive into the main directory:

```
ARJ x -jf -y DATA C:
```

The necessary directories will be created automatically and without any prompts. This is handled by the "-y" switch.

Damaged Archives

Occasionally, you may encounter an archive that cannot be decompressed. In this case, messages, such as "Broken archive", "Bad Data", "Bad Huffman code", "CRC-Error", and "Header damaged" appear. Regardless of the message that's displayed, the result is the same. These messages indicate that the archive is damaged in some way.

This is particularly frustrating when you can no longer access the original files. In this case, there is nothing you can do if the compression program doesn't have a function for repairing the damage.

Errors in the individual files are less serious. Although the file may be lost, the archive itself isn't in danger. The compression program usually indicates an error, if the CRC code of a file is no longer correct. During compression, this code is determined by file contents and saved in the archive. An error occurs when the CRC code, for some reason, no longer matches the original value.

Most of these errors are caused by faulty disk operations. However, even incompatible software cache programs can produce these errors.

As long as the archive is still intact, the damaged file can be removed. To do this, simply use the **Delete** command, which is included in every data compression program. First you must determine which file is damaged. If you didn't notice this during decompression, you should test the archive. Then you'll be able to identify the error.

All the compression programs use the same test command, "t":

```
PKUNZIP -t KAPUT
LHA t KAPUT
ARJ t KAPUT
```

To test the archive, the program decompresses it. However, instead of being written onto the disk, the decompressed data isn't written anywhere. The CRC code can be recalculated and compared with the stored value. Other discrepancies can also be discovered by using this method.

It can be dangerous to the entire archive if structural information, called the header, is changed. This header contains important information on the location, starting position, length, compression methods, etc. of the files. It's possible that all subsequent data will be lost if the header is unusable.

For example, if the file header of the third archived file is defective and, as a result, the file length cannot be determined, then it will no longer be possible to access the beginning of the next archived file.

A less serious problem involves compressed files that are defective. In this case, there isn't much danger to the archive. However, a defective data region can be disastrous, if an important document happens to be the one that's damaged.

Although PKZIP/PKUNZIP and ARJ have special functions for managing damaged archives, these programs cannot miraculously change bad files into good ones.

PKZIP/PKUNZIP and damaged archives

Use PKZIPFIX when PKUNZIP cannot decompress an archive because the headers are destroyed. PKZIPFIX reconstructs damaged information or finds the next header if the questionable header is completely unusable. PKZIPFIX works relatively successfully because the ZIP archives contain some structural information that isn't needed.

PKUNZIP has found errors in the archive

This program is very user-friendly because parameters are used. Simply enter the filename of the archive; the rest is automatic.

The program restores the file information so the decompression process can be performed. CRC errors and other discrepancies aren't removed. The final result is placed in a separate file called "PKFIXED.ZIP" instead the original KAPUT.ZIP file. Use the following command to decompress the file:

```
PKUNZIP PKFIXED
```

PKZIPFIX attempts to fix the damaged archive

If an archive was repaired with PKZIPFIX, use the data output by PKUNZIP carefully. Because of defective data, the files can be incorrectly decompressed and completely useless.

To check this data, we produced a test case. We copied a small text file (with legible contents) five times, archived it with PKZIP, and then changed the archive with a disk editor. As expected, PKUNZIP could no longer do anything with the archive and demanded PKZIPFIX.

PKZIPFIX seems to have taken care of the problem. But after decompressing the repaired archive again with PKUNZIP, it was obvious that the file information was no longer correctly decompressed. Instead of producing readable information, the file contained only garbage characters.

As you can see, make certain the decompressed files were correctly restored after decompressing damaged archives.

LHA and damaged archives

You can easily determine what was damaged by using the integrity test. For example, the KAPUT.LZH archive originally had seven files. However, after a test run, LHA suddenly reports something quite different:

```
LHA t KAPUT
```

```
C:\>LHA T KAPUT

Testing archive : KAPUT.LZH

Testing  CHAP07.DOC   oooo....
Broken archive.

C:\>
```

The archive is damaged

Of the seven files, only one remains and this file is defective. This is indicated by the "Decompressing marker." Not all the points in the circles are filled. This simply means that an error occurred in this archive in the middle of the decompression process.

Because of this error, the file header "CHAP07.DOC" was apparently overwritten. As a result, the files following it can no longer be located. The program displays the "Broken archive" message. If only the data region of the file is defective, the message "CRC Error" appears and the structure of the archive isn't destroyed. In this case, the only solution in LHA is to try to delete the damaged file. You may be able to do this because you know the name of the defective file, which is probably "CHAP07.DOC." Use the "d" command to delete this file:

```
LHA d KAPUT CHAP07.DOC
```

If the response to this command is "CHAP07.DOC Deleted", the operation was successful. However, if LHA still displays the message "Broken archive", the files are lost forever.

As you can see in the following illustration, our example operation was successful. The CHAP07.DOC file was deleted. To verify this information, run the integrity test, which provides the remaining files.

```
C:\>LHA T KAPUT

Testing archive : KAPUT.LZH

Testing  CHAP07.DOC   oooo....
Broken archive.

C:\>LHA D KAPUT CHAP07.DOC

Deleting from archive : KAPUT.LZH

Deleted  CHAP07.DOC

C:\>
```

The damaged file is deleted

58

Chapter 3

ARJ and damaged archives

In ARJ, use the decompression command with the "-jr" option", if header information is damaged and the ARJ archive can no longer be decompressed in the normal way with "e" or "x":

```
ARJ e -jr KAPUT
```

ARJ tries to find the local headers of the individual archives again, if it is no longer possible to locate the files in the archive on the basis of the available information.

"-jr" can be attached to all commands that aren't related to compressing files. So, you can't use this option with a-Add, u-Update, f-Freshen, and m-Move, for example.

If you use "-jr" with damaged files, at the end of the output, you may see a message indicating that ARJ has reached the end of the file unexpectedly. This occurs because ARJ no longer has information about the length of the file in the case of a damaged archive.

```
C:\>ARJ E -JR KAPUT
ARJ 2.41a Copyright (c) 1990-93 Robert K Jung. Jul 10 1993
*** This SHAREWARE program is NOT REGISTERED for use in a business, commercial,
*** government, or institutional environment except for evaluation purposes.

Processing archive: KAPUT.ARJ
Archive created: 1996-01-03 15:34:28, modified: 1996-01-03 15:34:28
Extracting DATA\WINWORD\CHAP07.DOC    to CHAP07.DOC    Bad file data, CRC error
!
Extracting DATA\WINWORD\CHAP05.DOC    to CHAP05.DOC    OK
Extracting DATA\WINWORD\CHAP04.DOC    to CHAP04.DOC    OK
Extracting DATA\WINWORD\CHAP03.DOC    to CHAP03.DOC    OK
Extracting DATA\WINWORD\CHAP01.DOC    to CHAP01.DOC    OK
Extracting DATA\WINWORD\CHAP02.DOC    to CHAP02.DOC    OK
     6 file(s)

Found     1 error(s)!

C:\>
```

Using the -jr option

PAK and damaged archives

PAK recognizes CRC errors and damaged header files. PAK also looks for and can even find headers, if the archive is not too badly damaged.

Compressing Your Data

4

Compressing Individual Files

As you've probably discovered while using your PC, files can quickly accumulate on your hard drive. These files can occupy valuable storage space. Eventually, your hard drive can become overloaded with all of these files. As a result, this slows the speed of your hard drive. Although you may use these files only occasionally, they may be too valuable to delete.

We'll discuss the basic compression commands in this chapter and provide examples that illustrate how to use these commands. You'll find all the information needed for compressing your data, from individual files to entire directories and their subdirectories. Since we'll discuss all the available compression programs, you should find information for the program you're using.

In this case, you can improve your hard drive's performance by using a data compression program to compress these files. Then simply delete the original uncompressed file from the hard drive. For example, suppose these files are located in a directory called "EXAMPLES." In this case, you would do the following:

1. Change to the EXAMPLES directory.

2. Create a compressed archive.

3. Delete the files that were archived.

First, enter the following to switch to the EXAMPLES directory:

```
CD\EXAMPLES
```

Now you can compress the files.

We used the PKZIP program in each example to keep them easy to understand. However, these procedures should apply to the other programs we discuss. You'll find a command reference for each program in Chapter 8.

If you're unfamiliar with the compression command, start the program's help function. To do this, simply enter the name of the program to see a list of the commands and switches:

PKZIP Enter

```
PKZIP (R)   FAST!   Create/Update Utility   Version 2.04g   02-01-93
Copr. 1989-1993 PKWARE Inc.  All Rights Reserved.  Shareware Version
PKZIP Reg. U.S. Pat. and Tm. Off.   Patent No. 5,051,745


PKZIP /h[1] for basic help   PKZIP /h[2|3|4] for other help screens.


Usage:  PKZIP [options] zipfile [@list] [files...]


        Simple Usage:   PKZIP zipfile file(s)...
                                    |     |     |
Program ------------------------    |     |
                                          |     |
New zipfile to create ----------------    |
                                                |
File(s) you wish to compress ----------

The above usage is only a very basic example of PKZIP's capability.


Press 2 for more options (including spanning & formatting), press 3 for
advanced options, 4 for trouble shooting options, any other key to quit help.
```

```
Usage:  PKZIP [options] zipfile [@list] [files...]

-a              Add files
-b[drive]       create temp zipfile on alternative drive
-d              Delete files
-e[x,n,f,s,0]   use [eXtra|Normal (default)|Fast|Super fast|NO compression]
-f              Freshen files
-l              display software License agreement
-m[f,u]         Move files [with Freshen | with Update]
-u              Update files
-p|P            store Pathnames|p=recursed into|P=specified & recursed into
-r              Recurse subdirectories
-s[pwd]         Scramble with password [If no pwd is given, prompt for pwd]
-v[b][r][m][t][c] View .ZIP [Brief][Reverse][More][Technical][Comment] sort by
  [d,e,n,o,p,s] [Date|Extension|Name|natural Order(default)|Percentage|Size]
-&[f|l|u]       Span disks [Format|format Low density|Unconditional format|
  u|w|v]            Unconditional Low density|Wipe disk|enable dos Verify|
  [s[drive]]        Back up entire disk w/ subdirs (-rp) [drive to back up]]

*** For more information, please consult the user manual ***
Press 1 for basic options, 3 for advanced options, 4 for trouble shooting
options, any other key to quit help.
```

```
Usage:  PKZIP [options] zipfile [@list] [files...]

-a+            clear archive Attribute after compression
-c             create/Edit Comments for all files
-C             add Comments for new files only
-i[-]          add files with archive Attribute set [don't turn attribute off]
-j!J<h,r,s>    mask!don't mask <Hidden/System/Read-only> files (default=jhrs)
-k             Keep original .ZIP file date
-o             set .ZIP file date to the latest file in .ZIP file
-q             enable ANSI codes in comments
-t[date]       take files NEWER than or EQUAL to date (default=today)
-T[date]       take files OLDER than date (default=today)
-w!W<h,s>      include!exclude <Hidden, System> files (default=Whs)
-x<file>       eXclude specified file
-x@list        eXclude file(s) in specified list file
-z             create or modify .ZIP comment
-!             add authenticity verification to .ZIP file (registered vers only)
-$[drive]      save Volume label in .ZIP file (default = current drive)
-@list         generate list file
-=             open file in compatibility mode (bypass share)
Press 1 for basic options, 2 for other options (including spanning and
formatting), 4 for trouble shooting options, any other key to quit help.
```

```
                -- TROUBLE SHOOTING OPTIONS --

If you experience difficulty with PKZIP, please consult your manual.
If problems continue, please document the problem as well as possible
and contact PKWARE technical support.

9025 North Deerwood Drive
Brown Deer, WI 53223

Support BBS: 414-354-8670
        Fax: 414-354-8559

-3             Disable 32-bit instruction usage on 80386 or higher CPU's
-^             Echo the command line
-+             Disable Expanded Memory (EMS) usage
--             Disable UMB/HMA Memory (XMS) usage
-~             Disable Network usage
-)             Disable 32 bit DPMI usage
-(             Use "Slow" MemCopy

Press 1 for basic options, 2 for other options (including spanning and
formatting), 3 for advanced options, any other key to quit help.
```

Four examples of the PKZIP Help screens

A list of optional switches appears in the lower portion of the Help screen. You must type the appropriate command or switch to create the archive.

From drive to archive

There are four ways to compress files. The most commonly used method involves adding files to an existing archive (**Add files to archive** command). If the archive doesn't exist, the compression program automatically creates it. The other compression methods provide a broader range of options. For example, the original files can be deleted automatically after they are compressed or only recently modified files can be included.

Command		Description
A	*Add files to archive*	Adds the indicated files to the archive. Previously archived files with the same name are overwritten.
M	*Move files to archive*	Similar to Add, but deletes the original files after the hard drive is compressed.
U	*Update files to archive*	Adds the indicated files to the archive, if they aren't already there or the archived version is older. This command ensures that your archive will always contain the most recent version of your files.
F	*Freshen files in archive*	The compression program refreshes the archive by looking for the most recent version of files on the hard drive. If it encounters a version of the file that was modified after a certain date, the newer version is added to the archive. It's impossible to create a new archive with Freshen.

All four commands can be used to add files in an existing archive. Now we'll explain how this process works. The command can either add individual files to an archive:

```
PKZIP -a ARCHIVE OBJECTS.TXT
```

or the command can add a group of files to an archive:

```
PKZIP -a ARCHIVE *.TXT
```

Update

There is only a minor difference between **Add** and **Update**. Both commands can create new archives if they don't exist yet and both commands compress files.

Unlike **Update**, **Add** archives a file regardless of whether it was already archived. So, you may accidentally overwrite a recent version of a file. This is true although the contents of the file being added are much older. **Update**, however, accepts only new and relatively recent files into the archive. If the archive isn't available when you use **Update**, it's created immediately.

```
ARJ -u TEXTS *.TXT
```

The above command adds a new document to the TEXTS archive only in the following:

❖ If it's not in the archive already

or

❖ If an older version of the file is in the archive

The **Update** command is included in all the compression programs that we describe. The following table shows the proper way to use this command in the different compression programs:

Update Command			
Program	Example	Program	Example
PKZIP	PKZIP -u ARCHIVE (File)	PKPAK	PKPAK -u ARCHIVE (File)
LHA	LHA u ARCHIVE (File)	PAK	PAK u ARCHIVE (File)
ARJ	ARJ u ARCHIVE (File)	ZOO	ZOO -add ARCHIVE (File)

Always use the Update command carefully. If the most recent version of the file is corrupt and you update an archive containing an older, noncorrupt file, you'll overwrite the older file. See Chapter 6 for more information on this problem.

Freshen

You can also use the **Freshen** command to update an archive. Considering the file date and timestamp, Freshen replaces files in an archive that are more recent. Unlike **Update**, only the files that are more recent than the ones already in the archive are accepted. Therefore, new files aren't archived.

The **Freshen** command can also create a new archive. The date and time the file was last saved determines whether the version of the file on the hard drive is more recent than the version in the archive. The archive contents shows the date and time listed for each file. The compression program compares the date and time of the archived file with the current file when compressing. It then accepts the newer one.

Use the **Freshen** command when you want to keep your archive current and organized and if you don't care about what the program may be adding to the archive.

We'll use an example to illustrate this. Suppose that you have an archive that contains only files of a certain type. This archive is called "PRESENT" and contains the files for a business presentation.

Now suppose that you make daily backups of the files for this project on the archive. By updating with **Freshen**, the compression program guarantees that only files already in the archive will be replaced by the new and current versions. The other files that were updated, but aren't related to your project, are not placed in the archive. Therefore, **Freshen** is extremely useful for filtering specific files.

> Since the Freshen command works automatically, you don't have to pay close attention to it. It only updates the files that are already in the archive.

If you use the **Freshen** command to update the archived files in TEXTS, use this command:

```
PKZIP -f TEXTS
```

If you want to update the entire archive you can omit "*.TXT" because new files won't be added to the archive. However, a file specification can be added to the end of the command. This is especially true when only specific files must be updated.

```
PKZIP -f TEXTS MEMO*.TXT
```

With the above command, all archived text files that have names starting with "MEMO" must be updated. All the other files in the archive aren't affected. New MEMO documents, which were written in the meantime, aren't archived with **Freshen**. In this case, you should use the **Update** command:

```
PKZIP -u TEXTS MEMO*.TXT
```

The following table shows how various data compression programs use the **Freshen** command:

Freshen Command			
Program	Example	Program	Example
PKZIP	PKZIP -f ARCHIVE (File)	PKPAK	PKPAK -f ARCHIVE (File)
LHA	LHA f ARCHIVE (File) LHA f -c ARCHIVE (File)	PAK	PAK f ARCHIVE (File)
ARJ	ARJ f ARCHIVE (File)		

LHA has the "-c" option which makes it possible to switch off the checking of the time marker. **Freshen** then works like **Add**, except that only files already in the archive are archived again.

Move

Move is a very useful command. However, use this command carefully because the original files are deleted after they are compressed. In PKZIP, the **Move** command looks as follows:

```
PKZIP -m TEXTS *.TXT
```

With the other compression programs, the **Move** command looks as follows:

```
LHA m TEXTS *.TXT

ARJ m TEXTS *.TXT

PKPAK -m TEXTS *.TXT

PAK m TEXTS *.TXT
```

To understand the above command lines, you must read them from the end of the line to the beginning. All the text files of the current directory are compressed in the TEXTS archive and then immediately deleted.

Changing the way Move works

In principle, **Move** works like **Add**. Files are archived even if the version in the archive is more current. However, it's possible to change this process. For example, suppose that you want to combine **Update** or **Freshen** with the deletion features of **Move**. You may want to check the archive before certain files are deleted. To change the way **Move** operates, you must add more options in the command line.

Using PKZIP to Update or Freshen and Delete

You can easily do this in PKZIP. If you want to use the **Move** command with **Update** or **Freshen**, enter the first letter of the corresponding command after the "-m" command:

```
PKZIP -mu TEXTS *.TXT        (Update + Delete)
PKZIP -mf TEXTS *.TXT        (Freshen + Delete )
```

PKPAK is just as easy following the same parameters:

```
PKPAK -mu TEXTS *.TXT        (Update + Delete)
PKPAK -mf TEXTS *.TXT        (Freshen + Delete )
```

Using ARJ to Update or Freshen and Delete

In ARJ, you can use the "-jt" parameter, which is a safety feature. If the compression operation was successful, all the archived text documents will be deleted only after an additional check is made. You should use the "-jt" option to protect your data.

```
ARJ m -jt WORDTXT *.TXT
```

If you want ARJ to prompt you for confirmation before deleting files, use the "-d" option. However, "-d" is used with **Add** instead of **Move**.

```
ARJ a -d TEXTS *.TXT
```

Now you know three ways you can "Move" files into an archive with ARJ:

```
ARJ m TEXTS *.TXT           (simple)
ARJ m -jt TEXTS *.TXT       (test first)
ARJ a -d TEXTS *.TXT (test query)
```

As we mentioned, **Move** works like the **Add** command. In other words, all the files are overwritten regardless of whether they're an older version of the file. However, this may not always be desirable and can be changed in many data compression programs.

Although ARJ cannot use the same parameters as PKZIP, it does have three switches that make this change even easier:

Switch	Purpose
-n	Only new files which have not yet been archived are accepted into the archive.
-f	Only recent files are archived. Corresponds to Freshen + Move.
-u	Only recent or new files are archived. Corresponds to Update + Move.

Instead of **Move**, it's also possible to use a combination of **Add** and "-d"-**Delete**. Therefore, you can use both

```
ARJ m -n TEXTS *.TXT
```

and

```
ARJ a -dn TEXTS *.TXT
```

to create a Move command that affects only text files that haven't been compressed.

Using LHA to Update or Freshen and Delete

LHA uses **Move** differently than the other compression programs. LHA automatically checks the file age and archives only recent and new files. So, LHA has a built-in Update feature, which you can switch off.

```
LHA m -c TEXTS *.TXT (Age isn't checked)
```

The "-c" option, which is also used with **Freshen**, ensures that the archive is renewed regardless of the age of the files.

Using ZOO to Update or Freshen and Delete

The ZOO program offers two variations of the **Move** command, which are useful for both beginners and experienced users. The following is the simple version of the command:

```
ZOO -move TEXTS *.TXT
```

69

This version is the same as the one used by the other compression programs. The more advanced version produces the same result but with increased compression.

```
ZOO aMP TEXTS *.TXT
```

The "a" represents the **Add** command. The additional command "M" (**Move**) deletes the original file and "P" (**Pack**) removes unnecessary (garbage) data. (Remember that the ZOO program is case-sensitive.) If you also add the "u" or "n" parameter to the above command, it's possible to use this method with **Freshen** and **Update**.

Additional parameters in ZOO

Switch	Purpose
n	Only new files, which have not yet been archived, are accepted into the archive.
u	Only recent or new files are archived. Corresponds to Update + Move.

The following table shows how **Move** can be used with the different compression programs:

Move Command		
Program	Command Line	Result
ARJ	ARJ m WORDDOC *.TXT ARJ m -jt ... ARJ a -d ... ARJ m -u ... ARJ m -f ... ARJ m -n ...	Default Move with supplementary test Move with query Move + Update Move + Freshen Move + Only-New-Files
LHA	LHA m WORDDOC *.TXT LHA m -c ...	Default with age comparison Move without file age
PKZIP	PKxxx -m WORDDOC *.TXT	Standard
PKPAK	PKxxx -mu WORDDOC *.TXT PKxxx -mf WORDDOC *.TXT	Move + Update Move + Freshen
PAK	PAK m WORDDOC *.TXT PAK m /WO ... PAK m /WA ...	Default with query Move with age comparison (Update) Move without comparison
ZOO	ZOO -more WORDDOC *.TXT ZOO -aMP ... ZOO -auMP ... ZOO -anMP ...	Default simple Default complicated Move + Update Move + Only-New-Files

Use the PAK program carefully. Even if files aren't "moved" into the archive, PAK still deletes them from your hard drive.

Listing archive contents

After compressing files, you should display the archive. You can quickly find the **List** command (command switch "-v") in the PKZIP Help file.

```
PKZIP -v SAMPLE
```

A list containing information about the files archived in SAMPLE appears:

```
C:\>PKZIP -v DATA1

PKZIP (R)    FAST!   Create/Update Utility    Version 2.04g    02-01-93
Copr. 1989-1993 PKWARE Inc.  All Rights Reserved.  Shareware Version
PKZIP Reg. U.S. Pat. and Tm. Off.    Patent No. 5,051,745

■ 80486 CPU detected.
■ XMS version 3.00 detected.
■ Novell Netware version 3.11 detected.
■ DPMI version 0.90 detected.

Searching ZIP: DATA1.ZIP

 Length  Method    Size  Ratio    Date    Time    CRC-32  Attr  Name
 ------  ------    ----  -----    ----    ----    ------  ----  ----
  65536  DeflatN  19006  71%   12-28-95  21:05  797b9c6b  --w-  CHAP07.DOC
  69120  DeflatN  19037  73%   12-28-95  21:05  4af353d1  --w-  CHAP05.DOC
  59392  DeflatN  18834  69%   12-14-95  15:38  dcf535ae  --w-  CHAP04.DOC
  72192  DeflatN  20175  73%   12-14-95  16:29  b544d017  --w-  CHAP03.DOC
  44544  DeflatN  15463  66%   12-14-95  14:46  1ba09ce2  --w-  CHAP01.DOC
  38400  DeflatN  10231  74%   12-15-95  09:38  6438ae19  --w-  CHAP02.DOC
 ------          ------  ---                                    --------
 349184          102746  71%                                        6

C:\>
```

The contents of the documents archive

The most interesting thing in this list is probably the compression ratio, which is listed for each file. The overall ratio for all the archived files results from the average of the individual rates.

PKZIP is one of the most effective data compression programs currently available. Remember, the compression ratio always depends on the file type.

Even larger compression ratios are possible, which proves how much compression programs can help you create space on your hard drive. The **List** commands for the other compression programs are located in the following table:

List Command			
Program	Example	Program	Example
PKZIP	PKZIP -V ARCHIVE (File)	PKPAK	PKPAK -V ARCHIVE (File)
LHA	LHA I ARCHIVE (File)	PAK	PAK I ARCHIVE (File)
ARJ	ARJ I ARCHIVE (File)	ZOO	ZOO -List ARCHIVE (File)

As you can see, it's easy to create and display archives. The commands of these file compression programs are very similar. Since PKZIP and PKPAK use the "V" parameter for list, you may get confused and accidentally type the "L" parameter. However, if this happens, don't worry. This parameter just displays the license information for your data compression program.

If you want to save the contents of an archive or print the contents, you can redirect the output to a file or to the printer instead of to the screen. To do this, enter the ">" sign after the command for listing an archive, followed by a filename or the printer interface (usually LPT1):

```
PKZIP -v SAMPLE > FILE
```

or

```
PKZIP -v SAMPLE > lpt1
```

The first command sends the output to a text file, which you'll be able to process like a normal text. The second command sends the archive contents to the printer.

File lists

To specify the files to be compressed, type either their complete filenames or use wildcards (* or ?). Entering these commands can be time-consuming, especially if you can't use wildcards. In this case, you must type the same command several times:

```
PKZIP -a PRESENT LAST.TXT
PKZIP -a PRESENT LETTER.BAK
PKZIP -a PRESENT DATA.DBF
PKZIP -a PRESENT TABLE.XLS
PKZIP -a PRESENT START.XLM
PKZIP -a PRESENT GRAPH.CHT
...
```

However, there is an easier way to do this. You can simply pass an entire list of files to the compression programs in a single command as in:

```
PKZIP -a PRESENT LAST.TXT LETTER.BAK DATA.DBF TABLE.XLS START.XLM GRAPH.CHT
```

This command line can also be combined with the other commands, such as "-v" for **List**.

You can also prepare a file list in advance. You can generate the file list with any text editor, even with the DOS editors EDIT or EDLIN. For a small file, even the COPY CON command is suitable:

```
COPY CON LIST
LAST.TXT
LETTER.BAK
DATA.DBF
TABLE.XLS
START.XLM
GRAPH.CHT

1 File(s) copied
```

Press ⌗F6⌗ to place an end-of-file character in the file and then close the file by pressing ⌗Enter⌗. Now the **Update** command, along with the list, is passed to the compression program. In PKZIP, this command looks as follows:

```
PKZIP -u @LIST
```

If you have several list files, these can also be entered more than once in the command line:

```
PKZIP -u @LIST @DOCS
```

To prevent confusion, PKZIP identifies a list file with the "At" symbol @ (ASCII character 64). Without this character in front of the filename, the compression program would compress the list file itself.

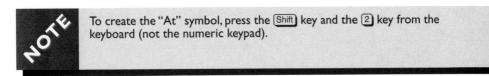
NOTE: To create the "At" symbol, press the ⌗Shift⌗ key and the ⌗2⌗ key from the keyboard (not the numeric keypad).

Only PKZIP and ARJ support list files.

PKZIP	(Command) ARCHIVE @LIST	Make certain the end-of-file character (^Z) doesn't appear in the last text line of the list file because this entry won't be recognized.
ARJ	(Command) ARCHIVE !LIST	The exclamation point represents the list file.

Any function that can work with more than one file can be used for "Command" in the above command lines.

LHA doesn't recognize the list files in this way. If you want to use predefined lists with this program, you'll have to use a trick. One of these tricks is called piping, which is used in DOS. With piping, you can redirect input and output channels. (We'll discuss piping in more detail in Chapter 6.)

Excluding files from an archive

Suppose that you've created a lot of files during the day. You want to compress all the files except for a few. You can do this one of two ways:

1. Compress all the files and then delete the unwanted ones from the archive. You'll learn how to do this in Chapter 4.

2. Specify which files should be excluded from the compression process during archiving.

PKZIP and ARJ have this exclusion capability. Both programs use the same switch to do this:

```
-x "File"
```

Use "-x" to specify that the subsequent filename shouldn't be bypassed by the program. The exclusion switch can also be used with the other commands, such as **Freshen**, **Update**, and **List**. You can use "-x" with commands which we haven't discussed yet, such as **Unpack** or **Delete Files in Archive**.

The following PKZIP example shows how all the files of a directory are archived, except for program files:

```
PKZIP -u SAMPLE -x*.exe -x*.com
```

All files, with the exception of the .EXE and .COM files, in the current directory are compressed and saved in the SAMPLE archive. As you can see from the example, each exclusion must be preceded by its own "-x".

74

The exception switch can also be combined with file lists:

```
PKZIP -u SAMPLE -x@PROGS
```

If the PROGS file still contains unnecessary entries, such as

```
*.COM
*.EXE
*.BIN
*.SYS
*.OVL
```

you can prevent them from finding their way into your archive program by using a simple exclusion list.

It's easy to confuse the "-x" switch of ARJ with the "x" command, which is used to decompress files (eXtract).

This confusion doesn't occur with PKZIP because, unlike the other compression programs, PKZIP uses a separate program, called PKUNZIP, for decompressing files. Unlike PKZIP, the PKUNZIP program doesn't let you exclude files.

Compressing Directories

Besides individual files, you can also compress entire directories. This makes it possible to build a complete "package", which can include several directories and subdirectories, into one archive. The directory structure needed to operate a specific program is later rebuilt.

How the subdirectory files are located depends on the compression program. Some programs cannot work with subdirectories. These compression programs are able to represent directories:

❖ PKZIP

❖ ARJ

❖ LHA

Recursive search

PKZIP, ARJ, and LHA use a recursive search to store files in directory trees. The compression process begins at the starting directory entered in the command line. First, all the files in that directory are compressed. Next, the compression program determines whether a subdirectory exists. If there is a subdirectory, the program jumps to this directory and begins processing these files. As with all recursion, only specified files are placed in the archive.

If entire directory trees are archived, the pathnames of the files are very important. The compression program must determine whether the files should be saved with the complete pathname. For example, there is a significant difference between archiving a file as

```
README.DOC
```

or

```
C:\BORLAND\TPASCAL\DOCDEMOS\README.DOC
```

If files are saved from many different directories, it's possible that two files with the same name would be compressed into the same archive. However, without a pathname, this isn't possible.

Another problem can also occur with archives that don't have complete paths. Because the pathnames are missing, the files may not be able to be restored to the proper directories when they are decompressed.

The following should help you decide if you should create an archive with a complete pathname:

With path data	Select this setting to ensure that the directory structure of the original is accurately backed up, or if some of the files have the same name.
File name only	This setting is sufficient if you only want to back up all files of a certain type within a directory tree.

The default setting used for saving the complete path is different in each compression program. ARJ automatically saves the complete path, while LHA and PKZIP do this only when specifically told to do so.

Using PKZIP

PKZIP has two switches that affect how files from different directories are handled:

-r	Recursive storage of files. If files with duplicate names are found in a subdirectory, they are passed over without further checking.
-p	Addition of directory names, into which a branch is made during the recursive search.
-P	Addition of the name of the starting directory and recursively branched directories.

The simplest way to use recursive archiving in PKZIP is a command with the "-r" switch:

```
C:\DATA\WINWORD\PKZIP -a -r ALLDOC *.DOC
```

PKZIP searches all subsequent subdirectories for files ending with "DOC" beginning with the current directory (in our example this is the C:\DATA\WINWORD directory). If the program encounters new files with a name that was already assigned, the file isn't archived.

```
C:\data\WINWORD>PKZIP -A -R ALLDOC.*.DOC

PKZIP (R)   FAST!   Create/Update Utility   Version 2.04g   02-01-93
Copr. 1989-1993 PKWARE Inc.   All Rights Reserved.   Shareware Version
PKZIP Reg. U.S. Pat. and Tm. Off.   Patent No. 5,051,745

■ 80486 CPU detected.
■ XMS version 3.00 detected.
■ Novell Netware version 3.11 detected.
■ DPMI version 0.90 detected.
■ Using Normal Compression.

Creating ZIP: ALLDOC.ZIP
  Adding: CHAP07.DOC    Deflating (71%), done.
  Adding: CHAP05.DOC    Deflating (73%), done.
  Adding: CHAP04.DOC    Deflating (69%), done.
  Adding: CHAP03.DOC    Deflating (73%), done.
  Adding: CHAP01.DOC    Deflating (66%), done.
  Adding: CHAP02.DOC    Deflating (74%), done.
  Adding: DISPLAY.DOC   Deflating (68%), done.
  Adding: EXCHANGE.DOC  Deflating (64%), done.
  Adding: CONFIG.DOC    Deflating (70%), done.

C:\data\WINWORD>
```

Simple recursive archiving with PKZIP

During this compression run, PKZIP finds 9 files in the directory tree. If the "p" switch is found on the command line, the path data of directories lying deeper within the directory structure are to be added to the filename.

```
PKZIP -a -rp ALLDOC *.TXT
```

The result of this search already looks slightly different. Both the filenames and the list of names are longer.

```
■ 80486 CPU detected.
■ XMS version 3.00 detected.
■ Novell Netware version 3.11 detected.
■ DPMI version 0.90 detected.
■ Using Normal Compression.

Updating ZIP: ALLDOC.ZIP
Updating: CHAP07.DOC          Deflating (71%), done.
Updating: CHAP05.DOC          Deflating (73%), done.
Updating: CHAP04.DOC          Deflating (69%), done.
Updating: CHAP03.DOC          Deflating (73%), done.
Updating: CHAP01.DOC          Deflating (66%), done.
Updating: CHAP02.DOC          Deflating (74%), done.
Updating: DISPLAY.DOC         Deflating (68%), done.
Updating: EXCHANGE.DOC        Deflating (64%), done.
Updating: CONFIG.DOC          Deflating (70%), done.
Updating: EXTRA/CHAP07.DOC    Deflating (71%), done.
Updating: EXTRA/CHAP05.DOC    Deflating (73%), done.
Updating: EXTRA/CHAP04.DOC    Deflating (69%), done.
Updating: EXTRA/CHAP03.DOC    Deflating (73%), done.
Updating: EXTRA/CHAP01.DOC    Deflating (66%), done.
Updating: EXTRA/CHAP02.DOC    Deflating (74%), done.

C:\data\WINWORD>
```

Archiving with pathnames

Instead of 9 files, 15 files were archived. Since the pathnames were also saved, the filename "FILE1.TXT" is no longer the same as "EXTRA\CHAP07.DOC". No other duplicate files are found.

Remember, the two "P" options are case-sensitive. The lowercase "p" controls files and pathnames in the current directory. However the uppercase "P" specified the directory stated in the command line. Both of these commands:

```
C:\DATA\WINWORD>PKZIP -a -rp ALLDOC *.DOC
```

and

```
C:\DATA\WINWORD>PKZIP -a -rp ALLDOC *.DOC
```

produce an identical result because there is no additional subdirectory. However, this isn't the case for these two commands:

```
C:\DATA\WINWORD>PKZIP -a -rp ALLDOC C:\DATA\WINWORD\ *.DOC
```

and

```
C:\DATA\WINWORD>PKZIP -a -rP ALLDOC C:\DATA\WINWORD\ *.DOC
```

78

The P command in the first version changes nothing without specific path data, because deviant directories (i.e., those named in the command line) aren't placed in the archive. The files in the first P command can be placed anywhere when they are decompressed. Only the files in subdirectories to C:\DATA\WINWORD get a path prefix. The files in the second P command must be decompressed under the C:\DATA\WINWORD directory. The difference in the P version can now be seen. Because there is a path specification here (C:\DATA\WINWORD*.DOC), it will be attached to all files found.

```
C:\>PKZIP -A -RP ALLDOC C:\DATA\WINWORD\EXTRA\*.DOC

PKZIP (R)   FAST!   Create/Update Utility   Version 2.04g   02-01-93
Copr. 1989-1993 PKWARE Inc.  All Rights Reserved.  Shareware Version
PKZIP Reg. U.S. Pat. and Tm. Off.   Patent No. 5,051,745

» 80486 CPU detected.
» XMS version 3.00 detected.
» Novell Netware version 3.11 detected.
» DPMI version 0.90 detected.
» Using Normal Compression.

Updating ZIP: ALLDOC.ZIP
Updating: DATA/WINWORD/EXTRA/CHAP07.DOC  Deflating (71%), done.
Updating: DATA/WINWORD/EXTRA/CHAP05.DOC  Deflating (73%), done.
Updating: DATA/WINWORD/EXTRA/CHAP04.DOC  Deflating (69%), done.
Updating: DATA/WINWORD/EXTRA/CHAP03.DOC  Deflating (73%), done.
Updating: DATA/WINWORD/EXTRA/CHAP01.DOC  Deflating (66%), done.
Updating: DATA/WINWORD/EXTRA/CHAP02.DOC  Deflating (74%), done.

C:\>
```

Complete path information for all files

Using LHA

Similar to PKZIP, LHA has a switch that controls recursive storage and another that specifies that pathnames will be saved:

-r	Recursive collection of files.
-x	Saving files with expanded name data.

These two options work with most command switches. Therefore, it's possible to add files to the archive by using **Update**, **Move** or **Freshen**. To implement recursive storage, use the -r switch.

```
LHA a -r ALLDOC \*.DOC
```

79

The above command archives all the backup files, of the current drive, that have the .DOC file extension. Press (Enter) to activate this command. The command may execute without any problems or a message similar to the following may appear:

```
C:\>lha a -r alldoc \*.doc

Creating archive : alldoc.LZH


Same names in another path : 'CHAP07.DOC'

C:\>
```

This message appears and LHA stops working when two files with the same name are met as you try to add them to the same archive. To avoid this problem, you must, in the case of LHA, add an "-x" option. With this switch, you're also adding the pathname to the filename. The result is that even files with the same name can be processed by LHA.

```
C:\>lha a -rx alldoc \*.doc

Creating archive : alldoc.LZH

==>   33% CHAP07.DOC    oooooooo
==>   34% CHAP05.DOC    ooooooooo
==>   34% CHAP04.DOC    oooooooo
==>   33% CHAP03.DOC    ooooooooo
==>   35% CHAP01.DOC    oooooo
==>   32% CHAP02.DOC    ooooo
==>   34% DISPLAY.DOC   oo
==>   37% EXCHANGE.DOC  o
==>   32% CONFIG.DOC    ooo
==>   33% CHAP07.DOC    oooooooo
==>   34% CHAP05.DOC    ooooooooo
==>   34% CHAP04.DOC    oooooooo
==>   33% CHAP03.DOC    ooooooooo
==>   35% CHAP01.DOC    oooooo
==>   32% CHAP02.DOC    ooooo

C:\>
```

Using recursive collection

As you can see in the above illustration, LHA doesn't display the path of a file, even if the path is saved. However, you can display the path information by using the "-l" parameter:

```
LHA u -rxl ALLDOC\*.DOC
```

Now the following will appear on the screen:

```
 ==> 33% oooooooooo
[5/15] /DATA/WINWORD/CHAP01.DOC
 ==> 35% oooooo
[6/15] /DATA/WINWORD/CHAP02.DOC
 ==> 32% ooooo
[7/15] /DATA/WINWORD/DISPLAY.DOC
 ==> 34% oo
[8/15] /DATA/WINWORD/EXCHANGE.DOC
 ==> 37% o
[9/15] /DATA/WINWORD/CONFIG.DOC
 ==> 32% ooo
[10/15] /DATA/WINWORD/EXTRA/CHAP07.DOC
 ==> 33% ooooooooo
[11/15] /DATA/WINWORD/EXTRA/CHAP05.DOC
 ==> 34% ooooooooo
[12/15] /DATA/WINWORD/EXTRA/CHAP04.DOC
 ==> 34% ooooooooo
[13/15] /DATA/WINWORD/EXTRA/CHAP03.DOC
 ==> 33% ooooooooo
[14/15] /DATA/WINWORD/EXTRA/CHAP01.DOC
 ==> 35% oooooo
[15/15] /DATA/WINWORD/EXTRA/CHAP02.DOC
 ==> 32% ooooo

C:\>
```

Path display during compression

Using ARJ

With ARJ, you don't have to worry about the path when compressing directories. ARJ automatically saves the directory names. If you don't want save the path names, you must specify this. Use the following parameters when working with directories:

-r	Recursively collects files in subdirectories.
-e	Saves filenames without path data.
-a1	Archives empty directories with the others.

By using a brief command, you can immediately save all files, along with their paths, in the archive:

```
ARJ a -r ALLDOC C:\DATA\WINWORD\*.DOC
```

To exclude paths in the archive, use the optional -e switch.

```
C:\>arj a -re alldoc c:\data\winword\*.doc
ARJ 2.41a Copyright (c) 1990-93 Robert K Jung. Jul 10 1993
*** This SHAREWARE program is NOT REGISTERED for use in a business, commercial,
*** government, or institutional environment except for evaluation purposes.

Creating archive  : ALLDOC.ARJ
Adding    C:\DATA\WINWORD\CHAP07.DOC    28.3%
Adding    C:\DATA\WINWORD\CHAP05.DOC    27.1%
Adding    C:\DATA\WINWORD\CHAP04.DOC    31.8%
Adding    C:\DATA\WINWORD\CHAP03.DOC    27.7%
Adding    C:\DATA\WINWORD\CHAP01.DOC    34.1%
Adding    C:\DATA\WINWORD\CHAP02.DOC    28.3%
Adding    C:\DATA\WINWORD\DISPLAY.DOC   33.2%
Adding    C:\DATA\WINWORD\EXCHANGE.DOC   37.2%
Adding    C:\DATA\WINWORD\CONFIG.DOC    31.1%
Adding    C:\DATA\WINWORD\EXTRA\CHAP07.DOC    28.3%
Adding    C:\DATA\WINWORD\EXTRA\CHAP05.DOC    27.1%
Adding    C:\DATA\WINWORD\EXTRA\CHAP04.DOC    31.8%
Adding    C:\DATA\WINWORD\EXTRA\CHAP03.DOC    27.7%
Adding    C:\DATA\WINWORD\EXTRA\CHAP01.DOC    34.1%
Adding    C:\DATA\WINWORD\EXTRA\CHAP02.DOC    28.3%
   15 file(s)

C:\>
```

Compressing with ARJ without path data

What appears on the screen can be misleading. Duplicate filenames appear on the screen, but just the filenames, not the paths, are saved in the archive. However, something is wrong with the previous compression procedure. The ARJ archive now contains several files with the same name. If you display the archive, you'll see the duplicate files.

```
*** government, or institutional environment except for evaluation purposes.

Processing archive: ALLDOC.ARJ
Archive created: 1996-01-04 13:45:42, modified: 1996-01-04 14:06:52
Filename      Original Compressed Ratio DateTime modified CRC-32   AttrBTPMGUX
------------- -------- ---------- ----- ----------------- -------- -----------
CHAP07.DOC       65536     18524  0.283 95-12-28 21:05:12 797B9C6B A--W B 1
CHAP05.DOC       69120     18700  0.271 95-12-28 21:05:12 4AF353D1 A--W B 1
CHAP04.DOC       59392     18914  0.318 95-12-14 15:38:00 DCF535AE A--W B 1
CHAP03.DOC       72192     20026  0.277 95-12-14 16:29:32 B544D017 A--W B 1
CHAP01.DOC       44544     15177  0.341 95-12-14 14:46:06 1BA09CE2 A--W B 1
CHAP02.DOC       38400     10868  0.283 95-12-15 09:38:18 6438AE19 A--W B 1
DISPLAY.DOC      15954      5290  0.332 95-07-11 09:50:00 E29C98B2 A--W B 1
EXCHANGE.DOC      7072      2633  0.372 95-07-11 09:50:00 C6ACF3CF A--W B 1
CONFIG.DOC       17752      5519  0.311 95-07-11 09:50:00 39065BF8 A--W B 1
CHAP07.DOC       45056     14888  0.330 96-01-04 14:06:38 A69BA40D A--W B 1
CHAP05.DOC       69120     18700  0.271 95-12-28 21:05:12 4AF353D1 A--W B 1
CHAP04.DOC       59392     18914  0.318 95-12-14 15:38:00 DCF535AE A--W B 1
CHAP03.DOC       72192     20026  0.277 95-12-14 16:29:32 B544D017 A--W B 1
CHAP01.DOC       44544     15177  0.341 95-12-14 14:46:06 1BA09CE2 A--W B 1
CHAP02.DOC       38400     10868  0.283 95-12-15 09:38:18 6438AE19 A--W B 1
------------- -------- ---------- -----
   15 files    718666    214224 0.298

C:\>
```

Duplicate files in the archive

The archive contains duplicate and multiple listings of the same files. For example, "CHAP07.DOC" appears twice. But you also see from the file sizes, dates, and times, that all the files are different. Therefore, files with the same names don't overwrite each other. It doesn't matter under which names the files are saved with ARJ.

When you decompress the ARJ archive, you must be careful with files that have the same name. If you decompress all files into a directory, several files having the same name cannot be placed in the same directory. So, these files would gradually be overwritten.

Empty directories

You're probably wondering why anyone would compress an empty directory. However, doing this is helpful because it saves you work when compressing a previously-installed program to an archive so you can move the program to a different computer. If you compress the empty directories needed by the program, these directories will be set up, according to the original structure, on the target computer when you decompress the archive. So, you won't have to reinstall all the directories or manually create the missing ones.

You can compress empty directories directly only with ARJ. With LHA and PKZIP, you must use a few tricks.

The command for ARJ is as follows:

```
ARJ a -r -al ALLDIR *.TXT
```

In the above line, an archive called "ALLDIR" will be created from all the files with the TXT file extension. "-al" ensures that any empty directories will also be backed up. Whether a file is hidden, is important for the system, or is actually a directory, can be determined from the file attribute, which is controlled by DOS.

Since neither PKZIP nor LHA support this attribute, you must do the following:

1. Determine which directories are empty.

2. Create a "dummy" file in each of these directories.

Although the name of this file isn't important, it must be the same in all empty directories. The easiest and fastest way to create this file is with COPY CON. Therefore, switch to the empty directory and enter:

```
COPY CON LITTLE.ONE
a  F6 Enter
```

The file is now complete. Its content is the letter "a" and the end-of-file character ^Z, which is created by pressing F6. You can place any letter in the file. However, remember that you cannot press F6 as the first key, because the file wouldn't contain anything and, therefore, wouldn't be created.

3. Repeat this process for each empty directory or simply copy the file to the appropriate directories.

Now you can compress the data. If you want to retain the directory structure along with the files (as in the ARJ example), the PKZIP command would be:

```
PKZIP -a -rp ALLDIR *.TXT *.ONE
```

or for LHA:

```
LHA a -r -x ALLDIR *.TXT *.ONE
```

With these "dummy" files, both compression programs will now also accept the empty directories (which aren't really empty) into the archive. You don't have to delete these files.

Editing Archives

It's important that you keep your archives well-organized. All the compression programs let you edit the archive once it's created. This involves updating and freshening the files of the archive, as we discussed earlier in this chapter. However, the most important commands for keeping your archives organized are **View**, **Delete**, and **Rename**.

Examining the archive

To maintain an archive, you must know what an archive contains. As we discussed in this chapter, the **List** command displays the contents of archives.

With all compression programs, the **List** command is entered with one or two letters and can be modified easily by using a switch. This switch determines how the list is displayed and what information is included.

84

Various kinds of information can be displayed with the **List** command. You can display a simple listing or very technical information, which provides an in-depth look into the archive.

Except for a few minor differences, using the **List** command provides the following information (in this or a similar format):

Filename	*Filename*	The number of all archived files is displayed in the last line.
Comment	*Comment*	If the file in the archive has its own comment, this is displayed. With most compression programs, this occurs automatically, but you'll have to activate it for each option.
Date/Time	*Date and time*	The original file date and time. On the basis of these dates, archives are updated (Update) or freshened (Freshen).
CRC	*CRC code*	The CRC (Cyclic Redundancy Check) code of a file is a key calculated from the contents of a file according to a complicated mathematical procedure. The correct compression of the data is checked with these codes.
Length	*Original file length*	The sum of all file lengths is displayed at the end of the table.
Size	*According to file length*	The total length of all compressed files is displayed at the end of the table.
	Compression	Compressed files shown.
Ratio	*Degree of compression*	This value shows by what percent the file size was decreased. Many compression programs also show the size of the compressed file as compared to the original (as a percentage). The average degree of compression is displayed at the end of the table.

```
C:\>lha -l lhasampl.lzh

Listing of archive : LHASAMPL.LZH

Name          Original    Packed  Ratio   Date       Time     Attr Type  CRC
------------  --------   --------  -----  --------   --------  ---- -----  ----
SAMPLE.TXT      291262      91564  31.4%  96-01-08  12:48:38  a--w -lh5-  AA5F
SAMPLE.PCX     1278248    1030243  80.6%  95-08-02  16:29:00  a--w -lh5-  7AAB
SAMPLE.TIF     1228546    1184942  96.5%  95-08-02  16:02:20  a--w -lh5-  1F9B
SAMPLE.EXE      309696     146520  47.3%  93-09-30  06:20:00  a--w -lh5-  74FC
SAMPLE.HLP     1914880    1638285  85.6%  95-02-01  00:00:00  a--w -lh5-  AABB
SAMPLE.DBF      860970     148390  17.2%  95-02-01  00:00:00  a--w -lh5-  CB65
SAMPLE.BMP     1282062     774518  60.4%  96-01-08  13:50:58  a--w -lh5-  EAD6
------------  --------   --------  -----  --------   --------
7 files        7165664    5014462  70.0%  96-01-08  16:50:26

C:\>
```

Using the (L)ist command in LHA to list files in the compressed file

PKZIP

PKZIP also provides a view command for examining the archive. Activate this command with the "-v" option:

```
PKZIP -v ZIPSAMPL.ZIP
```

The archive contents are displayed in the following format:

```
C:\>pkzip -v zipsampl.zip

PKZIP (R)    FAST!   Create/Update Utility    Version 2.04e    01-25-93
Copr. 1989-1993 PKWARE Inc.  All Rights Reserved.  Shareware Version
PKZIP Reg. U.S. Pat. and Tm. Off.    Patent No. 5,051,745

■ 80486 CPU detected.
■ XMS version 3.00 detected.
■ Novell Netware version 3.11 detected.

Searching ZIP: ZIPSAMPL.ZIP

Length  Method    Size  Ratio   Date      Time    CRC-32   Attr  Name
------  ------    ----  -----   ----      ----    ------   ----  ----
291262  DeflatN  81331   73%   01-08-96  12:48  28815b8b  --w-  SAMPLE.TXT
1278248 DeflatN 1012513  21%   08-02-95  16:29  889c18c7  --w-  SAMPLE.PCX
1228546 DeflatN 1182866   4%   08-02-95  16:02  6d518054  --w-  SAMPLE.TIF
309696  DeflatN 141387   55%   09-30-93  06:20  604bf3de  --w-  SAMPLE.EXE
1914880 DeflatN 1605876  17%   02-01-95  00:00  65500472  --w-  SAMPLE.HLP
860970  DeflatN 139403   84%   02-01-95  00:00  27cbc48f  --w-  SAMPLE.DBF
1282062 DeflatN 781419   40%   01-08-96  13:50  0cb808c3  --w-  SAMPLE.BMP
------          ------  -----                                   -------
7165664         4944795  31%                                          7

C:\>
```

Using the -v option to list archive contents

"V" is an abbreviation for VIEW. The distinction between a normal and detailed listing originates from other compression programs, which actually have two different List functions.

The PKZIP **List** command provides the option for viewing the contents in a text file. In its complete form, the command is:

```
PKPAK -eList (Name)
```

With the "-eList" option, the screen pauses briefly before the DOS prompt reappears. To display the output, type the following command:

```
PKPAK Name
```

You'll see the contents of the zipped file but without any comments or file information. This is handy for keeping track of the archived files.

LHA and ICE

There isn't much difference in how LHA and the completely compatible ICE display archives.

The difference involves two options. While "I" displays a simple list of archived files, "v" also includes the pathnames. This difference is important because LHA and ICE, unlike PKPAK, can also save files from subdirectories.

```
LHA v ARC
```

This command looks very similar to the PKZIP version. The output is divided into two parts because one screen line is always reserved for the path. Because of this, the listing is difficult to read.

If you don't want to display the pathnames of the files, use the short listing. To do this, use the "l" command instead of "v":

```
LHA l ARC
```

A plus sign appears at the beginning of the line if a file has a subdirectory.

```
sting of archive : ALLDOC.LZH

Name            Original     Packed  Ratio   Date       Time     Attr Type  CRC
--------        --------     ------  -----   --------   ------   ---- -----  ---
CHAP07.DOC         65536      21643  33.0%  95-12-28  21:05:12  a--w -lh5- 59DE
CHAP05.DOC         69120      23423  33.9%  95-12-28  21:05:12  a--w -lh5- 6EA7
CHAP04.DOC         59392      19918  33.5%  95-12-14  15:38:00  a--w -lh5- FEF5
CHAP03.DOC         72192      23804  33.0%  95-12-14  16:29:32  a--w -lh5- F121
CHAP01.DOC         44544      15657  35.1%  95-12-14  14:46:06  a--w -lh5- 65ED
CHAP02.DOC         38400      12323  32.1%  95-12-15  09:38:18  a--w -lh5- 2791
DISPLAY.DOC        15954       5442  34.1%  95-07-11  09:50:00  a--w -lh5- 0DE6
EXCHANGE.DOC        7072       2632  37.2%  95-07-11  09:50:00  a--w -lh5- 415D
CONFIG.DOC         17752       5664  31.9%  95-07-11  09:50:00  a--w -lh5- C45A
CHAP07.DOC         65536      21643  33.0%  95-12-28  21:05:12  a--w -lh5- 59DE
CHAP05.DOC         69120      23423  33.9%  95-12-28  21:05:12  a--w -lh5- 6EA7
CHAP04.DOC         59392      19918  33.5%  95-12-14  15:38:00  a--w -lh5- FEF5
CHAP03.DOC         72192      23804  33.0%  95-12-14  16:29:32  a--w -lh5- F121
CHAP01.DOC         44544      15657  35.1%  95-12-14  14:46:06  a--w -lh5- 65ED
CHAP02.DOC         38400      12323  32.1%  95-12-15  09:38:18  a--w -lh5- 2791
--------        --------     ------  -----   --------   ------
15 files          739146     247274  33.5%  96-01-04  13:39:44
\>
```

Short listing of an LHA archive

LHA and ICE don't provide a Pause function. If the listing is too long, the output scrolls over the screen rapidly. To pause the display, press Ctrl+S.

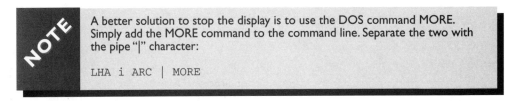

A better solution to stop the display is to use the DOS command MORE. Simply add the MORE command to the command line. Separate the two with the pipe "|" character:

```
LHA i ARC | MORE
```

This character is produced by simultaneously pressing Shift+\.

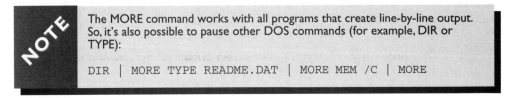

The MORE command works with all programs that create line-by-line output. So, it's also possible to pause other DOS commands (for example, DIR or TYPE):

```
DIR | MORE TYPE README.DAT | MORE MEM /C | MORE
```

Temporary directories

Compression programs occasionally run slowly. This is particularly noticeable when files have been archived directly onto diskettes or must be freshened or updated on diskettes.

Chapter 4

The reason for the slowdown in speed is that diskettes are accessed more slowly than hard drives. However, this isn't directly related to creating and processing archives. For example, working copies must be created, processed, copied, and again deleted to use **Freshen** or **Update**. These are time-consuming processes when using a diskette.

The working copy (compression programs also call it a temporary archive) is usually also created where the archive is located. This can lead to problems with memory space. Therefore, there won't be enough space for a working copy on a 1 Meg archive on a diskette.

To eliminate these waiting periods and avoid memory problems, you should swap the archive copy onto the hard drive. Simply add another parameter to the command line.

```
PKZIP -b(directory)
PAK   -b(directory)
PKPAK -b(directory)
LHA
ARJ   -w(directory)
```

The directory for the temporary archive is attached directly to the option letters without a space separating them.

```
PKZIP -f -bC:\ B:TEXTS *.TXT
LHA f -wC:\ B:TEXTS *.TXT
ARJ f -wC:\ B:TEXTS *.TXT
PKPAK -f -bC:\ B:TEXTS *.TXT
```

The directory must exist; otherwise the compression program will stop working. So, you should use the root directory. Since temporary archives must be deleted again immediately after the end of the operation, there is no danger that your root directory will gradually be filled with garbage data.

Another way to speed up this process is to use a RAM disk, which is a simulated drive. One part of your memory is split off to function like a drive. You can access this drive just like any real drive. However, remember that the data on the RAM disk will be lost as soon as you switch off the computer.

The advantages of a RAM disk are obvious. Because all operations take place directly in main memory, this temporary work place is faster than even the hard drive. You can always use this command, if your RAM disk is large enough.

To install a RAM disk, add the following line to the CONFIG.SYS file:

```
DEVICE=C:\DOS\RAMDRIVE.SYS 512 /E
```

This installs a driver called "RAMDRIVE.SYS" and activates it in your DOS directory. The RAM disk will have a size of 512K and use extended memory (/e).

The RAM disk automatically receives the next letter in the alphabet as its drive designation after your last hard drive. For example, if you have drives C:, D:, and E:, the RAM disk will automatically be drive F:. In this case, the commands for the compression program will be:

```
PKZIP -a -rP -bF: TABLES \*.XL?
ARJ a -r -wF: TABLES \*.XL?
LHA a -rxl -wF: TABLES \*.XL?
```

PKZIP

PKZIP includes many parameters for controlling output. If you access PKZIP's help function, you'll see an entire line of complete listing information:

```
-v[b,c,d,e,n,p,s,r,t]
```

Unfortunately, this line is confusing. You can reorganize the options so that they make sense:

```
-v[b,t,c] [d,e,n,p,s] [r]
```

These letters represent the first letter of each option.

PKZIP provides three different types of lists which you can control via the first parameter group. If you don't use one of these parameters, you'll get the default format, which is similar to the ones used by LHA and PKPAK.

Switch	Effect
b	Display of the list in short form (brief). The CRC value and the file attributes aren't displayed. Now the filenames and the path will fit on the screen.
t	Technical display format. Each file produces almost an entire screen page of information. (technical format).
c	Supplementary display of individual comments.

The options are used for sorting the list. Normally, the list isn't sorted without additional entries. The files are displayed in the sequence in which they were archived.

Parameter	Sort by	Parameter	Sort by
d	Date, Time	p	Percent of compression
e	Extension	s	Size
n	Name of the file	r	Reverse sorting

Like LHA, PKZIP doesn't have a switch for stopping the output when the screen is full. Therefore, in this case (as in the case of LHA) use the detour via the DOS command MORE.

```
PKZIP -v ALLDOC | MORE
```

The parameters can be combined in any way. However, PKZIP must be able to understand this arrangement. For example, there is nothing wrong with the following List command:

```
PKZIP -vbcpr ALLDOC
```

This command lists the archive in the short form (brief) with all the comments, sorting in reverse order in terms of the percentage of compression.

In this way, it's possible to arrange the list in any order. However, you'll receive the greatest amount of information if you select the technical format with the "t" option. This format can also be combined with sorting:

```
PKZIP -vt | MORE
```

ARJ

The two commands used for listing in ARJ are "l" and "v". The difference between these two commands is that the listing with "v" also displays the saved pathname for filenames and the current number in the archive.

```
ARJ l ALLDOC
```

The listing looks different from the other listings.

```
*** government, or institutional environment except for evaluation purposes.

Processing archive: ALLDOC.ARJ
Archive created: 1996-01-04 13:45:42, modified: 1996-01-04 14:06:52
Filename        Original Compressed Ratio DateTime modified CRC-32   AttrBTPMGVX
-------------- --------- ---------- ----- ----------------- -------- ---- -------
CHAP07.DOC         65536      18524 0.283 95-12-28 21:05:12 797B9C6B A--W B 1
CHAP05.DOC         69120      18700 0.271 95-12-28 21:05:12 4AF353D1 A--W B 1
CHAP04.DOC         59392      18914 0.318 95-12-14 15:38:00 DCF535AE A--W B 1
CHAP03.DOC         72192      20026 0.277 95-12-14 16:29:32 B544D017 A--W B 1
CHAP01.DOC         44544      15177 0.341 95-12-14 14:46:06 1BA09CE2 A--W B 1
CHAP02.DOC         38400      10868 0.283 95-12-15 09:38:18 6438AE19 A--W B 1
DISPLAY.DOC        15954       5290 0.332 95-07-11 09:50:00 E29C98B2 A--W B 1
EXCHANGE.DOC        7072       2633 0.372 95-07-11 09:50:00 C6ACF3CF A--W B 1
CONFIG.DOC         17752       5519 0.311 95-07-11 09:50:00 39065BF8 A--W B 1
CHAP07.DOC         45056      14888 0.330 96-01-04 14:06:38 A69BA40D A--W B 1
CHAP05.DOC         69120      18700 0.271 95-12-28 21:05:12 4AF353D1 A--W B 1
CHAP04.DOC         59392      18914 0.318 95-12-14 15:38:00 DCF535AE A--W B 1
CHAP03.DOC         72192      20026 0.277 95-12-14 16:29:32 B544D017 A--W B 1
CHAP01.DOC         44544      15177 0.341 95-12-14 14:46:06 1BA09CE2 A--W B 1
CHAP02.DOC         38400      10868 0.283 95-12-15 09:38:18 6438AE19 A--W B 1
-------------- --------- ---------- ----- ----------------- -------- ---- -------
   15 files       718666     214224 0.298

C:\>
```

File list with ARJ

The column with the rather strange heading BTPMGVX contains important information about the archived file. These letters have the following meaning:

Letter	Meaning
B	The file is a backup file.
T	Type of file: T Text B Binary D Directory
P	The file contains path information.
M	Compression method from 1 (basic) to 4 (rapid).
G	File was encoded with a key (garbled).
V	The following parts of the file are on other disks.
X	The file is a part of a larger file.

If a plus sign (+) appears in front of a file date, this indicates that a file is from the 21st century. Any file whose date doesn't begin with "19" is displayed this way. You don't have to scroll through long file lists when using ARJ. The "-jp" option halts the display of the list before it can run off the screen.

```
ARJ l -jp ALLDOC
```

ZOO

ZOO contains the "-List" command. It lets you easily display an archive:

```
ZOO -L ALLDOC
```

It's also possible to display several files at once. Since the ZOO archive normally attaches the .ZOO file extension, the following command line is sufficient:

```
ZOO -l *.ZOO
```

All archives found in the current directory will be displayed in sequence. Normally the faster commands are used instead of the more complex commands. So, "- List" is used as a fast version of the more complicated "VC" command. The following commands and modifiers can be used for listing files:

Modifier	Effect
L	Displays the standard table, in which the usual information about archived files is displayed.
V	The file information is displayed. Any comments are displayed.
v	File information is displayed. Similar to the "V" parameter but only the archive comments are displayed. Comments about individual files are suppressed. The letter "C" indicates that the file has a comment.
C	Displays the CRC code.

```
C:\>zoo -L alldoc

Archive alldoc.zoo:
Length    CF  Size Now  Date         Time
--------  --- --------  ----------   --------
   44544  53%    21253  14 Dec 95 14:46:06 65ed  /data/winword/chap01
   38400  57%    17326  15 Dec 95 09:38:18 2791  /data/winword/chap02
   72192  53%    33959  14 Dec 95 16:29:32 f121  /data/winword/chap03
   59392  53%    28040  14 Dec 95 15:38:00 fef5  /data/winword/chap04
   69120  52%    33569  28 Dec 95 21:05:12 6ea7  /data/winword/chap05
   65536  55%    30400  28 Dec 95 21:05:12 59de  /data/winword/chap07
   17752  55%     8077  11 Jul 95 09:50:00 c45a  /data/winword/config
   15954  53%     7547  11 Jul 95 09:50:00 0de6  /data/winword/displa
    7072  49%     3599  11 Jul 95 09:50:00 415d  /data/winword/exchan
--------  --- --------  ----------   --------
  389962  53%   183770   9 files

C:\>
```

Modifier Effect

93

Self-extracting Archives

The system operators (or sysops) of the many bulletin board systems were the first to use self-extracting archives. These operators placed the data that must be sent to the bulletin board users directly into a self-extracting archive. This helped them avoid many problems caused by users not having the proper version of a compression program in order to extract the necessary data.

Although the file sizes increased because of the automatic compressing, the amount of confusion and frustration among

Self-extracting archives are extremely helpful because they make it easier to distribute data to others. Not only can you transfer entire directory structures, the person receiving this data doesn't need a specific compression program. Perhaps what is more important, the person doesn't need to even understand data compression.

A normal archive file requires a specific compression program. However, a self-extracting archive simply needs its start command. This command is usually its name. So, these archives are easy to use.

In this chapter we'll discuss self-extracting archives created by PKZIP from PKWARE, ARJ and LHA.

users was drastically reduced. Today, self-extracting archives are widely used.

Self-extracting archives are also called "SFX archives." We'll use this abbreviation when discussing these archives in this chapter.

Structure of SFX archives

The structure of an SFX archive is actually quite logical. One part is the actual archive, which is built by the data compression program in the usual way, and the other part is the decompressor for the archive.

The decompressor portion is basically the algorithm, which is also used in the actual compression program, in decompression mode. The most important goal of an archive is to save as many bytes as possible.

Obviously, it wouldn't make sense to use compression methods that squeeze out every last bit of room and then cancel this out by using an elaborate SFX portion that requires a great deal of space.

The individual SFX modules (i.e., the portions of the file responsible for automatically decompressing the archive) are significantly different from one another. This is true in performance as well as in length (performance usually has a negative effect on length).

These "mini-modules" are often capable of amazing results. For example, with some SFX files, it's possible to display the contents or update the file without using the compression program.

It's also possible to treat an SFX archive like a normal archive and simply not worry about decompression. So, the following command is acceptable:

```
PKZIP -u ALLDOC.EXE *.TXT
```

With the above command, the compression program isn't concerned about the archive stuffed into the SFX module. Therefore, it's also possible to execute other operations, for which no provision is made in the self-extracting archive.

Using Self-Extracting Archives

By now you know that an SFX archive is able to decompress itself onto a storage medium. When decompressing archives, you must determine whether a function is already built into the compression program or is implemented as a separate program. LHA and ARJ use the built-in function.

The other data compression programs use self-sufficient programs to make a simple archive into a self-extracting archive. You can identify these programs by their names, such as ZIP2EXE and MAKESFX.

Most data compression programs also include the option of determining whether the SFX module should be large and powerful (with many options) or as small as possible.

When only a limited amount of space is available, it's possible to create the best setup. However, small SFX modules don't have any expanded capabilities, such as decompressing directory structures or updating list functions.

SFX archives and PKZIP

As we've mentioned, PKZIP uses many external programs to perform essential functions. Therefore, PKUNZIP is responsible for decompressing the archive. The ZIP2EXE program, in the PK group, creates self-extracting archives. The purpose of this program is indicated by its name, which stands for "from ZIP to EXE." Its only task is to attach an SFX module to a ZIP archive. To distinguish this module from other SFX modules, it's called "PKSFX."

To use the ZIP2EXE program, simply pass the name of the archive to the program:

```
ZIP2EXE Archive[.ZIP] [SFX archive]
```

Use the following command to convert an archive into a PKSFX archive:

```
ZIP2EXE HELLO
```

If a file extension isn't entered, ZIP2EXE assumes you mean a ZIP archive. So, in the above example, a HELLO.EXE archive is created from the HELLO.ZIP archive. It's also possible to create an SFX file, with a different name, from an archive:

```
ZIP2EXE HELLO AUTOMAT.EXE
```

The actual HELLO.ZIP archive isn't transformed. Similar to LHA, a supplementary PKSFX archive is created. This archive can be treated like a normal ZIP file. In this way, a PKSFX is similar to the SFX archives of an ARJ or LHA. Subsequent updating or freshening of a PKSFX is simple:

```
PKZIP -f AUTOMAT.EXE
```

The above command replaces all files in the AUTOMAT.EXE archive with "new" versions, if any are available. The only difference relative to working with "normal" ZIP archives is that the .EXE file extension must appear in the command line; otherwise PKZIP assumes you want to work on a ZIP archive.

PKSFX archive options

Although a PKSFX module increases the size of the archive by only about 13,000 bytes, it includes many options. To display these options, activate the Help function, which is included with every PKSFX module. To do this, enter the filename, followed by a "/?".

These options let you control which files should be decompressed from the self-extracting archive. You can also specify that files with the same name should be overwritten or necessary directories created.

Option	Effect
-n	Overwrites only older files that are present.
-o	Overwrites all files that have the same name.
-d	Creates directories, if they are needed.

These are the same options used with PKZIP and PKUNZIP. Even the command for testing the archive is available. Simply enter the filename, followed by "-t" as you can see in the following figure:

```
C:\>alldoc -t

PKSFX (R)   FAST!   Self Extract Utility   Version 2.04g  02-01-93
Copr. 1989-1993 PKWARE Inc. All Rights Reserved. Shareware version
PKSFX Reg. U.S. Pat. and Tm. Off.

Searching EXE: C:/ALLDOC.EXE
Testing: DATA/WINWORD/CHAP07.DOC   OK
Testing: DATA/WINWORD/CHAP05.DOC   OK
Testing: DATA/WINWORD/CHAP04.DOC   OK
Testing: DATA/WINWORD/CHAP03.DOC   OK
Testing: DATA/WINWORD/CHAP01.DOC   OK
Testing: DATA/WINWORD/CHAP02.DOC   OK
Testing: DATA/WINWORD/DISPLAY.DOC   OK
Testing: DATA/WINWORD/EXCHANGE.DOC   OK
Testing: DATA/WINWORD/CONFIG.DOC   OK
Testing: DATA/WINWORD/EXTRA/CHAP07.DOC   OK
Testing: DATA/WINWORD/EXTRA/CHAP05.DOC   OK
Testing: DATA/WINWORD/EXTRA/CHAP04.DOC   OK
Testing: DATA/WINWORD/EXTRA/CHAP03.DOC   OK
Testing: DATA/WINWORD/EXTRA/CHAP01.DOC   OK
Testing: DATA/WINWORD/EXTRA/CHAP02.DOC   OK

C:\>
```

Testing a PKSFX archive

Since all PKSFX archives can be used with PKZIP or PKUNZIP, other functions from these programs are also available. For example, if saved directory structures should be restored automatically, this is easily done with the PKSFX archive.

98

To do this, enter the "-d" switch in the command line, similar to decompressing normal ZIP archives:

```
"Filename"-d C:\PROJECT\BOSS\
```

With the above command, all files in the ALLDOC.EXE archive are decompressed into the C:\PROJECT\BOSS directory. The "-d" switch ensures that the necessary directories are created.

SFX archives and ARJ

It's easy to create self-extracting archives with ARJ.

As the only program with this capability, ARJ can provide its archive with the SFX module during compression. However, even a complete, normal archive can be equipped with the automatic decompressing function. The other data compression programs also operate according to this principle.

By adding the following parameters to the normal ARJ command lines, you can control the creation of SFX archives:

Parameter	Meaning
-je	An SFX archive is created during compression.
-je1	A small SFX archive is created during compression.
y	The SFX supplement is added to a completed archive.

You can create SFX archives by using all the functions that create normal archives, such as **Add**, **Update**, and **Move**.

```
ARJ u -je DBFS C:\DBASE\*.DB?
```

The above command collects all databases in the dBASE directory on the C: drive and archives them in the SFX archive DBFS. A normal archive is not created with this command (i.e., an archive without the decompressor). Only the .EXE archive is created.

To obtain both a normal ARJ archive, as well as the SFX archive, first you must create a normal archive. This archive is then "SFX-ized" with the "y" option:

```
ARJ u DBFS C:\DBASE\*.DB?    (Creates the archive)
ARJ y -je DBFS        (Creates the supplementary SFX archive)
```

The SFX option "je" can also be used with directory options. Therefore, you can combine entire tree structures, which are then placed on the target drive.

```
ARJ u -r -a1 -je -jf C:\ALLDOC A:\*.*
```

With the above command, all files and directories (even if they are empty) on the diskette in drive A: are transferred into the SFX archive "TOTAL" on the hard drive. The "jf" option ensures that the files are saved with their complete path data. To decompress the archive onto another diskette, simply start the SFX archive.

```
ALLDOC B:\
```

All the entries contained in this archive are decompressed onto drive B:. However, before a file is taken from the archive, ARJ first asks you to confirm whether decompression should begin:

```
C:\>alldoc
ARJSFX 2.41a - ARJ Archive Self-Extractor. ALLDOC.EXE -? for help.
Copyright (c) 1990-93 Robert K Jung. All Rights Reserved.

Processing archive: C:\ALLDOC.EXE
Archive date      : 1996-01-04 13:45:42
Continue extraction? y
```

This prompt appears whenever an SFX archive is started. You can respond with "Yes", "No", or "Quit". During decompression, ARJ always checks whether safety concerns are being impaired, and interrupts the process if files are overwritten or directories must be created.

100

```
Uncompressing      17752 bytes, OK
CHAP07.DOC   exists, Overwrite? y
Extracting CHAP07.DOC
Uncompressing      45056 bytes, OK
CHAP05.DOC   is same or newer, Overwrite? y
Extracting CHAP05.DOC
Uncompressing      69120 bytes, OK
CHAP04.DOC   is same or newer, Overwrite? y
Extracting CHAP04.DOC
Uncompressing      59392 bytes, OK
CHAP03.DOC   is same or newer, Overwrite? y
Extracting CHAP03.DOC
Uncompressing      72192 bytes, OK
CHAP01.DOC   is same or newer, Overwrite? y
Extracting CHAP01.DOC
Uncompressing      44544 bytes, OK
CHAP02.DOC   is same or newer, Overwrite? y
Extracting CHAP02.DOC
Uncompressing      38400 bytes, OK
    15 file(s)

*** NOT LICENSED for distribution use ***

C:\>
```

Safety prompts are included with SFX decompression

You can use the YES option "y" so that all prompts will be automatically confirmed. So, it's possible to have automatic decompression while suppressing all prompts:

```
ALLDOC -y B:\
```

ARJSFX features

With approximately 15,000 bytes, the SFX module of ARJ (abbreviated as ARJSFX) is rather large. However, it provides various options and is very powerful. For information about these SFX options, use the ARJSFX Help option "?". For example, to display information about the SFX archive created above, simply enter:

```
ALLDOC /?
```

The following Help screen appears:

```
C:\>alldoc /?
ARJSFX 2.41a - ARJ Archive Self-Extractor, ALLDOC.EXE -? for help.
Copyright (c) 1990-93 Robert K Jung. All Rights Reserved.

Usage: ARJSFX [-command] [-switch(s)] [directory\] [file(s)]

Commands:
e: Extract files              v: Verbosely list contents
l: List contents              x: eXtract files with pathname (default)
t: Test contents

Switches:
a: show ANSI comments         n: only New files
c: skip time stamp Check      p: match with Pathname
f: Freshen existing files     s: Skip security check
g: unGarble with password     u: Update files
i: no progress Indicator      y: assume Yes on queries

For information about the self-extracting portion of this software, contact:
ARJ Software, Robert K Jung, 2606 Village Road West, Norwood, MA 02062, USA

C:\>alldoc /?
```

Displaying information about ARJSFX options

NOTE An important difference between the normal ARJ compressor and the SFX archive is that a dash "-" must appear before commands and switches. This ensures that individual files with single-letter names, such as E or X, can be decompressed.

The commands are used as with normal decompression. So it's easy to list or test the archive:

```
ALLDOC -t
```

Only one command switch may appear in the line. However, it's possible to use other switches. For example, the following command displays all the files in the archive named "CHAP07":

```
ALLDOC -l CHAP07.*
```

This is possible because ARJ automatically saves files with their path information or archives files that have the same name. Use the "-P" option to change the display:

```
ALLDOC -l -p CHAP07.*
```

Now files that have only "CHAP07" in their path information will be displayed. This includes the CHAP07.BAK or CHAP07.STY file. However, it does not include the \DATA\WINWORD\CHAP07.DOC file.

When updating or freshening, the files in the archive are updated. With the ARJSFX module, use the following switches to determine which files on the target disk should be replaced by archived files:

Switch	Function
-u	Update (new + newer)
-n	Only missing files (new)
-f	Only recent files (freshen)

These options are the same as the ones used during normal decompression. With the following command, you can decompress the ALLDOC archive into the current directory. Older files are overwritten without any prompts, and missing files are added.

```
ALLDOC -u -y
```

This command is equivalent to the ARJ version:

```
ARJ x -u -y ALLDOC.EXE
```

What was created by ARJ can also be canceled. Although it's possible to decompress an SFX archive, delete the .EXE archive, and convert the uncompressed data into a normal archive again, this isn't necessary. Instead, simply use the **Join** "j" command:

```
ARJ j NEW ALLDOC.EXE
```

This command links archives. In the above example, the ALLDOC archive is "bound" to the NEW archive. The result is a normal NEW.ARJ.

You can combine almost any archives by using the **Join** command. For example, you can create an SFX archive that contains all the smaller SFXs.

Suppose that you archive all your diskettes and create ten individual SFX archives, DISK0 through DISK9, from these diskettes.

```
ARJ u -r -je -jf C:\DISKx A:\*.*
```

In this case, you'll have ten archives in the root directory of the hard drive. With a simple command (join) you can bind these archives together into a single SFX archive:

```
ARJ j -je ALLDISK DISK?.EXE
```

When you delete the individual archives, you'll save 135,000 bytes. This occurs because, for each archive, 15,000 bytes are needed for the SFX module. Now you only have to do that once.

ARJ's mini mini-module

The short version of the SFX module is called ARJSFXJR. With 5,400 bytes, this SFX module is significantly smaller than the ARJSFX module. As a result, it doesn't include the familiar functions of the larger SFX module.

Although it supports directory structures, ARJSFXJR doesn't display a prompt if a new directory must be created. Instead, it automatically does this. Also, if files of the same name are in the target directory, the files are overwritten.

With these capabilities, the mini-SFXJR module is ideal for passing data to others because the recipient doesn't have to know anything about archiving. However, even if he/she does know how to use the ARJ compression program, it isn't difficult to process an SFXJR module.

SFX archives and LHA

LHA also includes a built-in function for creating self-extracting archives. Unfortunately, LHA cannot directly create .EXE archives. LHA generates an SFX archive with the "s" switch:

```
LHA s EASY *.TXT
```

However, when you activate this command, the following error message appears:

```
C:\>lha s easy *.doc
Archive not found : 'easy.LZH'
C:\>
```

This is can be confusing, since the help information indicates that the "s" switch makes a self-extracting archive. However, it's easy to figure out why LHA refuses to run: LHA cannot generate an SFX file while compressing data. Therefore, the sequence of operations must be: First archive, then .EXEcute. In other words, first you must produce a normal LHA archive using the familiar capabilities of LHA. For example, if we use the example in which text files must be packed into an archive called "EASY.LZH", the entry would be as follows:

```
LHA u EASY *.TXT
```

Only then is the "self-decompressor", as these archives are called, created with the "s" option:

```
LHA s EASY
```

Other options aren't necessary. Now the following message appears instead of an error message:

```
C:\>lha s easy

Making SFX of archive : EASY.LZH

Extract   CHAP07.DOC
Extract   CHAP05.DOC
Extract   CHAP04.DOC
Extract   CHAP03.DOC
Extract   CHAP01.DOC
Extract   CHAP02.DOC
Extract   DISPLAY.DOC
Extract   EXCHANGE.DOC
Extract   CONFIG.DOC

C:\>
```

Then all archived modules are inserted into the SFX module.

LHA's SFX modules

LHA can produce two different versions of the SFX module. The smaller module is automatically used if the "s" switch is used without additional options. However, you can use the following options when creating the SFX archive:

Option	Effect
-x0	Default. Produces the small SFX module.
-x1	Creates the SFX module with expanded capabilities.

The smaller module stores files in an archive and can decompress these files in a target directory. This module doesn't work with directories. Also, the smaller SFX module cannot determine whether a file should be overwritten to update or freshen it. When a file with the same name appears in the target directory, LHA-SFX displays a prompt.

The SFX module is very small, which is shown by a small file conversion. For example, ALLDOC.LZH has a size of 248,199 bytes. After conversion, the result looks like this:

```
C:\>lha s alldoc

Making SFX of archive : ALLDOC.LZH

Extract   CHAP07.DOC
Extract   CHAP05.DOC
Extract   CHAP04.DOC
Extract   CHAP03.DOC
Extract   CHAP01.DOC
Extract   CHAP02.DOC
Extract   DISPLAY.DOC
Extract   EXCHANGE.DOC
Extract   CONFIG.DOC
Extract   CHAP07.DOC
Extract   CHAP05.DOC
Extract   CHAP04.DOC
Extract   CHAP03.DOC
Extract   CHAP01.DOC
Extract   CHAP02.DOC

C:\>
```

The SFX archive is only 1,225 bytes larger. Compared with the SFX module of LHA, this is extremely small. You can also bind the SFX module into the archive. As we mentioned, use the "-x1" switch to do this:

```
LHA s -x1 TOTAL
```

If you compare the larger archive with the normal file, the result is amazing:

```
C:\>dir alldoc

 Volume in drive C is C_DRIVE
 Volume Serial Number is 201A-1EE9
 Directory of C:\

ALLDOC   LZH      248,199  01-04-96  1:39p ALLDOC.LZH
ALLDOC   EXE      249,424  01-04-96  3:57p ALLDOC.EXE
        2 file(s)        497,623 bytes
        0 dir(s)     505,380,864 bytes free

C:\>
```

Although the features can't compare with the large SFX module of LHA, 1,225 bytes are much smaller than 34,283 bytes.

Functions of the LHA SFX module

This small module doesn't provide as many commands as ARJ's module. For example, this module doesn't include a help function. However, the large SFX module does support the restoration of directory structures. With this option, you can send data retrieved from the archive to any location on the hard drive.

```
ALLDOC C:\PRODUCT\DATA
```

Automatic batch files

LHA also provides a batch file that starts immediately after a large LHASFX archive is decompressed. This file is often called a "telop." In earlier versions of LHA, this file was called "AUTOLARC.BAT." In order for the batch file to start, the following requirements must be met:

1. The SFX module must be created with -x1 (therefore, it's an expanded module).

2. The telop file must be called !.BAT.

3. The SFX archive must be started with the "-!" option.

There are many uses for a telop. For example, you can send the following message to an inexperienced user after an archive is decompressed:

```
@ECHO OFF
CLS
ECHO Bravo, the files are now safe and sound on your hard disk.
ECHO Unfortunately, a tiny error has
ECHO crept in!
ECHO.
ECHO Switch off the screen IMMEDIATELY,
ECHO duck, put your head between your knees and
ECHO protect your neck with your hands.
ECHO RIGHT NOW!!!

ECHO Then count to two hundred and seek
ECHO the help of an expert.

ECHO If none comes, Good Luck!
ECHO.
ECHO Your Data Provider, B. Nice
```

Regardless of how you use the telop, remember the requirements: You must create the SFX archive with the "-x1" switch, call the telop file "!.BAT", and start the archive with the "-!" supplementary switch. If one of these requirements isn't fulfilled, the batch file won't be executed.

```
ALLDOC -!   (Unpacks the SFX archive and then starts !.BAT)
```

> You cannot use tricks to avoid these requirements. For example, if a !.BAT file is located in the target directory, this still won't work. The telop file must be in the archive, because it will be decompressed if the "-!" was entered as the switch.

Either !.BAT is executed (with the "-!" switch) or it is decompressed (without the switch). In the latter case, the batch file isn't started.

SFX archives and PAK

It's as easy to create a self-extracting archive with PAK. The EXEMAKE program converts a PAK archive into an SFX archive.

The information presented above for ZIP2EXE, from the PK family, also applies to EXEMAKE. Simply enter the name of the archive in the command line directly after the conversion command. For example:

```
EXEMAKE ALLDATA
```

Unless additional entries are made, PAK assumes the following:

❖ The archive is a PAK file (in our example, ALLDATA.PAK).

❖ The SFX file receives the same filename and the .EXE extension (in our example, ALLDATA.PAK becomes ALLDATA.EXE).

❖ Decompression occurs in the current directory.

PAK can also work with ARC archives created by PKPAK or the ARC data compression program. If you want to convert such a file into an archive capable of running, the name of the file extension must be specified. This is also true when the SFX file shouldn't have the same name as the archive.

```
EXEMAKE TEXTS.ARC ARCTEXT.EXE
```

In the above command, the -foreign ARC file becomes the self-extracting ARCTEXT.EXE.

An option is then permitted by the executable PAK archive. You can specify the target directory, if you finally decompress the SFX archive.

```
ARCTEXT C:\WORD\DOCUS
```

> However, the target directory must exist because new directories aren't created. Existing files with the same name aren't overwritten during decompression. Instead, the SFX module prompts you for permission.

PKPAK deviates somewhat from the simple way of constructing SFX archives.

As you learned earlier, a self-extracting file contains two parts, the actual file and a module, which contains the decompression algorithm.

The data compression program (or the appropriate external program, such as EXEMAKE or ZIP2EXE) now generates such an SFX module, copies the archive, and combines the two. This process is as follows:

1. Generate SFX module.

2. Copy archive.

3. Combine the two parts.

4. Then name the result "Filename".EXE.

PKPAK saves itself a lot of work. However, you must use the DOS command COPY / B because you must create an .EXE file. However, don't worry. This doesn't involve programming the SFX module with a program like GW-BASIC. Instead, you must start with the second step listed above.

The SFX module is contained in the PKPAK package. It has the name PKSFX.PGM and must be linked to the archive.

However, the module isn't available. So, you must create it yourself with the MAKESFX program. This program creates the PKSFX module and tailors it to your needs. Simply start MAKESFX and follow the directions:

```
MAKESFX
```

This procedure must be performed only once. When the PKSFX.PGM module is created, you can immediately start to create the self-extracting archive.

Combining SFX archives

If both the SFX module and the archive are available, simply copy the two parts together into a program. Use the COPY command:

```
COPY /b PKSFX.PGM+ARCHIVE.ARC ARCHIVE.EXE
```

The COPY command can be used to combine files. To do this, use the plus sign. In the above example, the PKSFX.PGM file is added to the ARCHIVE.ARC and the result is saved in the ARCHIVE.EXE file.

To ensure that the program will run, follow these guidelines:

1. Copy the two parts in the proper sequence. For example, the command "COPY ARCHIVE.ARC+PKSFX.PGM" isn't allowed.

2. Combine only true PKPAK archives with the SFX module.

3. Don't forget the "/B" option when copying.

The "/b" option ensures that the entire file will be copied.

A batch file is useful here. With this file, the self-extracting archive is created easily.

You can simply type this file in your text editor (Norton Commander, EDIT, EDLIN, etc.) and activate it with ARC2EXE.BAT:

```
@ECHO OFF
ECHO.

REM Test of option, and whether files are valid.

IF %1x==x GOTO Error
IF NOT EXIST %1.ARC GOTO Not_there
IF NOT %2x==x IF EXIST %2.EXE GOTO Already_there_2
IF EXIST %1.EXE GOTO Already_there_1

REM Create_the_file
```

```
ECHO Create target file ...
IF 2%x==x COPY /b PKSFX.PGM+%1.ARC 1%.EXE>NUL
IF NOT 2%==x COPY /b PKSFX.PGM+1%.ARC 2%.EXE>NUL
ECHO File created.
GOTO end

REM Error messages

:Error
ECHO ARC2EXE - Creates self-extracting archive
ECHO from PKPAK archive.
ECHO.
ECHO Application:
ECHO     ARC2EXE archive [Target archive]

ECHO.
ECHO  Tip:
ECHO     The extensions must not be entered,
ECHO     otherwise the program will not run correctly.
ECHO.
ECHO  Examples:
ECHO     ARC2EXE TEST          - Creates the TEXT.EXE FILE from TEXT.ARC
ECHO     ARC2EXE FIRST NEW     - Creates NEW.EXE from FIRST.ARC
GOTO end

:Not_there
ECHO Error!!!
ECHO The file %1.ARC cannot be found, processing terminated.
GOTO end

:Already_there_1

ECHO Error!
ECHO The target file %1.EXE is already present, processing terminated.
GOTO end

:Already_there_2
ECHO Error!
ECHO The target file %2.EXE is already present, processing terminated.

:end
ECHO.
```

This program is self-explanatory, if you read the comments after each REM command. The tests at the beginning of the file are very important. These tests check whether the archive and the target file exist. If ARC2EXE finds an error, the program is interrupted. The COPY command contains two lines because it's also possible to create SFX archives with different names.

Identifying SFX Archives

A confusing aspect of working with SFX archives is distinguishing them from other EXE programs. Obviously, just because a program is an EXE file doesn't automatically mean that it's a self-extracting archive.

One characteristic that all SFX archives, whether produced by ARJ or LHA, have in common is they all can be processed with the compression program. Normal programs, in other words, .EXE files without archive content, cannot be processed.

Suppose the active directory contains three programs which could be identified as SFX archives. Use the DIR command to display these files:

```
DIR *.EXE
```

```
C:\>dir.exe

 Volume in drive C is C_DRIVE
 Volume Serial Number is 201A-1EE9
 Directory of C:\

ALLDOC   EXE     236,137  01-04-96  4:14p ALLDOC.EXE
INSTALL  EXE      80,529  09-27-90  4:33p INSTALL.EXE
EASY     EXE     126,195  01-04-96  3:35p EASY.EXE
         3 file(s)       442,861 bytes
         0 dir(s)    506,331,136 bytes free

C:\>
```

Now you can begin testing the files to determine which ones are SFX archives. For our example, we'll use PKUNZIP. The easiest test is to check the potential archive with the **Test** command:

```
PKUNZIP -t EASY.EXE
```

113

After you press Enter, the test results appear:

```
C:\>pkunzip -t install.exe

PKUNZIP (R)     FAST!    Extract Utility    Version 2.04g  02-01-93
Copr. 1989-1993 PKWARE Inc. All Rights Reserved. Shareware Version
PKUNZIP Reg. U.S. Pat. and Tm. Off.

■ 80486 CPU detected.
■ XMS version 3.00 detected.
■ DPMI version 0.90 detected.

Searching ZIP: INSTALL.EXE
PKUNZIP: (W04) Warning! INSTALL.EXE - error in ZIP use PKZipFix

PKUNZIP: (E11) No file(s) found.

C:\>
```

The same result occurs with EASY.EXE. As you can see in the following illustration, only the INSTALL.EXE file is an SFX archive:

```
Copr. 1989-1993 PKWARE Inc. All Rights Reserved. Shareware Version
PKUNZIP Reg. U.S. Pat. and Tm. Off.

■ 80486 CPU detected.
■ XMS version 3.00 detected.
■ DPMI version 0.90 detected.

Searching ZIP: ALLDOC.EXE
Testing: CHAP07.DOC     OK
Testing: CHAP05.DOC     OK
Testing: CHAP04.DOC     OK
Testing: CHAP03.DOC     OK
Testing: CHAP01.DOC     OK
Testing: CHAP02.DOC     OK
Testing: DISPLAY.DOC    OK
Testing: EXCHANGE.DOC   OK
Testing: CONFIG.DOC     OK
Testing: EXTRA/CHAP07.DOC  OK
Testing: EXTRA/CHAP05.DOC  OK
Testing: EXTRA/CHAP04.DOC  OK
Testing: EXTRA/CHAP03.DOC  OK
Testing: EXTRA/CHAP01.DOC  OK
Testing: EXTRA/CHAP02.DOC  OK

C:\>
```

Identifying SFX archives

Although this method works, using a batch file would be easier. The following batch file, called "TESTSFX.BAT", checks whether a specific .EXE file is an SFX file:

114

```
@ECHO OFF
REM
REM TESTSFX.BAT
REM Checks whether a file is an LHA SFX file
REM
If %1x==x GOTO End
IF not exist %1 GOTO Not_there

PKZIP t %1
IF ERRORLEVEL 1 GOTO Not_an_archive
ECHO The file %1 is an SFX archive
GOTO End

:Not_an_archive
ECHO %1 is not a PKZIP archive
GOTO End

:Not_there
ECHO File %1 not found.
GOTO End

:End
ECHO.
```

The actual testing takes place in the "PKZIP t %1" line.

If you're dealing with only one file, you can test this file just as quickly by activating the compression program.

Now suppose that you want to test several .EXE files to determine whether they are associated with various data compression programs. To do this, you must divide the program into two batch files. The first file, IsSFX.BAT, determines the filenames and associates them with the different compression programs. The second file, PTEST.EXE, is the actual test file:

```
@ECHO OFF
REM
REM ISSFX.BAT
REM
:Tests
  IF %1x==x GOTO Error
  IF Exist %1 GOTO individually

:Group
  IF %1x==/ex FOR %%V IN (*.EXE) DO CALL PTest %%V
  IF %1x==/Ex FOR %%V IN (*.EXE) DO CALL PTest %%V
  GOTO End
```

```
:Individually
  CALL PTest %1
  GOTO End

:Error
  ECHO.
  ECHO IsSFX - Determines whether a program is an SFX archive.

  ECHO.
  ECHO    Application: ISSFX (file) or /e
  ECHO       ISSFX  P.EXE        - checks P.EXE
  ECHO       ISEXE  /e           - checks all .EXE files in the
  ECHO                             directory
  ECHO       ISSFX               - This Help screen
  ECHO.
  ECHO    Tip:
  ECHO       The program reports only inconsistencies,
  ECHO       not error messages.
:End
  ECHO.
```

Although this looks very complicated, it really isn't. The file consists of five parts. Each part tests for a specific compression program. Each of these parts performs the same steps:

1. Calls the **Test** command, along with the file to be checked.

2. Checks whether an error has occurred.

3. In the case of an error, the program concludes that the file isn't an archive. The program then jumps to the next test with GOTO. If an error didn't occur, a message, indicating that the file could be an archive, is displayed.

This structure makes it easy to include a new compression program. Simply insert this command into the file before the ":PEnd" line and change the line with the call to this compression program. For example, to incorporate the (hypothetical) compression program NEWPAK, enter the following:

```
...
...
:TPKPAK
  PKPAK -t %1 > NUL
  IF ERRORLEVEL 1 GOTO PEnd
  CTTY CON
  ECHO    %1 seems to be a PKPAK archive.
```

116

```
* GOTO TNewPAK

REM *** here comes the new part ***

:TNewPAK
* NEWPAK test %1 > NUL
* IF ERRORLEVEL 1 GOTO PEnd
  CTTY CON
* ECHO   %1 seems to be a  NEWPAK archive.
  GOTO PEnd

:PEnd
CTTY CON
```

Asterisks precede the lines that have been changed. However, this program still isn't adequate because it checks only a specific file, whose name must be entered. Now the starting file, IsSFX.BAT, which takes over the rest of the work, is needed to check all the .EXE files of a directory.

```
REM
REM PTEST.BAT
REM
@ECHO OFF
ECHO %1
CTTY NUL

:TARJ
  ARJ t %1 > NUL
  IF ERRORLEVEL 1 GOTO TLHA
  CTTY CON

  ECHO   %1 seems to be an ARJ archive.
  GOTO PEnd

:TLHA
  LHA t %1 > NUL
  IF ERRORLEVEL 1 GOTO TPKZIP
  CTTY CON
  ECHO   %1 seems to be an LHA archive.
  GOTO PEnd

:TPKZIP
  PKUNZIP -t %1 > NUL
  IF ERRORLEVEL 1 GOTO TPKPAK
  CTTY CON
  ECHO   %1 seems to be a PKZIP archive.
  GOTO PEnd
```

```
:TPKPAK
  PKPAK -t %1 > NUL
  IF ERRORLEVEL 1 GOTO notSFXarchive
  CTTY CON
  ECHO    %1 seems to be a PKPAK archive.
  GOTO PEnd

:notSFXarchive
  CTTY CON
  ECHO   %1 does not seem to be a SFX archive.
  GOTO PEnd


:PEnd
CTTY CON
```

Don't let the length of the program intimidate you. The program is easy to use. If you want to check an individual file, activate the batch file as follows:

```
ISSFX ALLDOC.EXE
```

To check several files, call IsSFX.BAT without filenames, but with the "/E" option:

```
ISSFX /E
```

Checking files with the ISSFX program

Tips On Self-Extracting Archives

Although SFX archives are easy to use, you should be aware of a few things. In this section, we'll give you some tips on working with self-extracting archives.

Root directories

It's extremely important that the root directory of your hard drive is well-organized. Since the root directory has only a limited amount of space, unnecessary files should be deleted or moved to other directories.

The reason for this space restriction is that the root directory belongs to the system region of the hard drive. This region can contain only 512 entries. So, the root directory cannot contain more than 512 files or directories. Although this may seem like a lot, an archive can include numerous files, which quickly fill up the root directory.

If the root directory is completely filled, no other files can be decompressed. If this occurs, you must delete these files from the root directory. This is easy to do with files that have the same extension but if the archive contains a variety of files, this can be very confusing.

The system files of the root directory may also be overwritten. The following files are especially at risk:

❖ COMMAND.COM

and

❖ CONFIG.SYS

It's possible that these files will be replaced by files that aren't compatible with your system. If this occurs, your computer may stop working. Because of this possibility, remember that you should always have a backup system diskette available.

119

Advanced Data Compression Features

Password Protection

Since the original files cannot be restored without the compression program that was used to compress them, archives are actually encrypted data.

However, to protect an archive completely, you should protect it with a password. The password you type "locks" the compressed data within the archive. Later, the data cannot be uncompressed until the same password is entered to unlock it. Therefore, a password-protected archive is doubly encrypted: Once by compression and again by password locking. The process of uncompressing reverses these steps to decrypt the data into its original form.

Today's file compression programs provide an overwhelming variety of features. You've probably discovered this if you've ever used "PKZIP /?" to display the entire PKZIP help screen. The few commands needed for normal use are hidden by switches, abbreviations, punctuation and comments.

Therefore, we began this book by explaining the basics of file compression. Now we'll discuss the advanced data compression features. We'll start with the functions included in most compression programs and then discuss special functions that are found in only certain programs.

Some programs provide more options than others. By reading about their capabilities, you can choose the compression program that is best for you.

Scrambling and garbling

Scrambling and garbling are two different methods of locking archived files by using a password. An abbreviation indicates which method the program used. Working with passwords is always optional. When included, a password follows the associated command.

Passwords can be used with all commands that involve compressing or uncompressing archives:

Add, Update, Freshen, Move / Extract / Test

You cannot use a password with a command such as List or View because these functions only display filenames. The archive itself isn't affected. Some compression programs, however, display an indicator to show whether an archived file is password-protected.

```
 DPMI version 0.90 detected.

Searching ZIP: ALLDOC.ZIP

 Length  Method    Size  Ratio    Date      Time    CRC-32   Attr  Name
 ------  ------   ------  -----   -------   -----   --------  ----  ----
  65536  DeflatN   19018   71%   12-28-95   21:05   797b9c6b  --w-*  CHAP07.DOC
  69120  DeflatN   19037   73%   12-28-95   21:05   4af353d1  --w-   CHAP05.DOC
  59392  DeflatN   18846   69%   12-14-95   15:38   dcf535ae  --w-*  CHAP04.DOC
  72192  DeflatN   20187   73%   12-14-95   16:29   b544d017  --w-*  CHAP03.DOC
  44544  DeflatN   15463   66%   12-14-95   14:46   1ba09ce2  --w-   CHAP01.DOC
  38400  DeflatN   10231   74%   12-15-95   09:38   6438ae19  --w-   CHAP02.DOC
  15954  DeflatN    5262   68%   07-11-95   09:50   e29c98b2  --w-*  DISPLAY.DOC
   7072  DeflatN    2610   64%   07-11-95   09:50   c6acf3cf  --w-   EXCHANGE.DOC
  17752  DeflatN    5475   70%   07-11-95   09:50   39065bf8  --w-   CONFIG.DOC
  65536  DeflatN   19006   71%   12-28-95   21:05   797b9c6b  --w-   EXTRA/CHAP07.DOC
  69120  DeflatN   19037   73%   12-28-95   21:05   4af353d1  --w-   EXTRA/CHAP05.DOC
  59392  DeflatN   18834   69%   12-14-95   15:38   dcf535ae  --w-   EXTRA/CHAP04.DOC
  72192  DeflatN   20175   73%   12-14-95   16:29   b544d017  --w-   EXTRA/CHAP03.DOC
  44544  DeflatN   15463   66%   12-14-95   14:46   1ba09ce2  --w-   EXTRA/CHAP01.DOC
  38400  DeflatN   10231   74%   12-15-95   09:38   6438ae19  --w-   EXTRA/CHAP02.DOC
 ------           ------   ---                                      -------
 739146           218875   71%                                         15

C:\>
```

PKZIP indicates password-protected files

PKZIP displays password-encrypted files with an asterisk on the normal view screen. The technical view option

```
PKZIP -vt SECRET
```

displays an additional text notation (although it's difficult to see) for such files.

Entering the password

A file is password-protected at the time it is compressed. That is why passwords apply to commands that involve the archiving process (Move, Add, Update, Freshen). The password itself can be considered an additional parameter for the command.

PKZIP uses "s" (scrambling), ARJ, PAK, and PKPAK use the "g" option (garbling). Both parameters have the same syntax:

```
PKZIP -u -sABACUS SECRET  C:\DATA\WINWORD
```

The password parameter immediately follows the other command parameters needed for file archiving. A space isn't inserted between the other parameters and the password parameter. For example:

```
PKZIP -u -s ABACUS SECRET C:\DATA\WINWORD ( *** wrong!!!  )

PKZIP -u -sABACUS SECRET C:\DATA\WINWORD ( that's better )
```

This also applies to other programs, as you can see from the following table. The table shows some differences in the way the programs recognize the password option. For PKPAK, the password parameter isn't separated from the other command parameters (in this case, "u" for update). Adding a space causes an error.

Command	Case sensitive	Command	Case sensitive
PKZIP -a -sHELLO Archive	yes	PKPAK -agHELLO Archive	no
ARJ u -gHELLO Archive	yes	PAK u /gHELLO Archive	no

With passwords, PKZIP/PKUNZIP and ARJ are case-sensitive. This means that these programs distinguish between uppercase and lowercase characters. So you must remember exactly how you type the password when you lock a file, and use the same capitalization when unlocking it later. To these programs, "HELLO" is a different password than "Hello." PKPAK and PAK, however, aren't case-sensitive. These programs don't distinguish between upper and lowercase characters.

You don't have to use the same password to encrypt every file within an archive. Each file can have its own unique password. However, it would be difficult to remember all these passwords. Also, the archiving process would be very time-consuming because each password must be entered on its own command line, such as:

```
PKZIP -u -sPetER SECRET *.TXT

PKZIP -u -sANnA SECRET *.DBF

PKZIP -u -sX23oSS SECRET RECIPE.GHM
```

The above example uses three different passwords to compress several files into a common archive called "SECRET." Since PKZIP distinguishes between upper and lowercase characters in passwords, you must remember exactly how you entered each password. Of course, you could write down each password, but this defeats the purpose of using passwords.

ARJ allows you to hide the password while you type it so that no one can see the password on the screen. To hide your entry, type a question mark, instead of a password, directly after the "g" parameter. ARJ requests the password, which will be blanked out on the screen as you type it. For example, if you enter the following command

```
ARJ u -g? NEWARCH C:\DATA\WINWORD\*.DOC
```

ARJ will respond with the following message:

```
C:\>arj u -g? newarc c:\data\winword\*.doc
ARJ 2.41a Copyright (c) 1990-93 Robert K Jung. Jul 10 1993
*** This SHAREWARE program is NOT REGISTERED for use in a business, commercial,
*** government, or institutional environment except for evaluation purposes.

Enter garble password:
Re-enter password to verify:
Creating archive  : NEWARC.ARJ
Adding    C:\DATA\WINWORD\CHAP07.DOC    28.3%
Adding    C:\DATA\WINWORD\CHAP05.DOC    27.1%
Adding    C:\DATA\WINWORD\CHAP04.DOC    31.8%
Adding    C:\DATA\WINWORD\CHAP03.DOC    27.7%
Adding    C:\DATA\WINWORD\CHAP01.DOC    34.1%
Adding    C:\DATA\WINWORD\CHAP02.DOC    28.3%
Adding    C:\DATA\WINWORD\DISPLAY.DOC   33.2%
Adding    C:\DATA\WINWORD\EXCHANGE.DOC  37.2%
Adding    C:\DATA\WINWORD\CONFIG.DOC    31.1%
    9 file(s)

C:\>
C:\>
```

If you make a mistake while entering the password, you obviously cannot see it on the screen. So, you'll be prompted to enter the password again to verify that it is correct.

Accessing protected archives

Passwords actually lock the individual files within an archive, not the archive itself. So, a protected archive is subject to some degree of access, even if all of its data cannot be extracted.

If you forget a password, only files encrypted with that particular password are lost. Any other files stored in the same archive can still be extracted. The password itself isn't stored in the archive. Instead, it is used by a mathematical algorithm in the CRC (Cyclic Redundancy Check) calculation. Encrypted files are followed by unencrypted ones.

Chapter 6

Note that only the first files are locked. When you try to extract archived data, the program doesn't tell you if you enter an incorrect password. It simply reports a CRC error.

```
ARJ e -ghello SECRET
```

```
C:\>arj x -g? newarc
ARJ 2.41a Copyright (c) 1990-93 Robert K Jung. Jul 10 1993
*** This SHAREWARE program is NOT REGISTERED for use in a business, commercial,
*** government, or institutional environment except for evaluation purposes.

Enter garble password:
Processing archive: NEWARC.ARJ
Archive created: 1996-01-05 11:15:10, modified: 1996-01-05 11:15:10
ARJ      65536 95-12-28 21:05:12, DISK     65536 95-12-28 21:05:12
DATA\WINWORD\CHAP07.DOC    is same or newer, Overwrite? y
Extracting DATA\WINWORD\CHAP07.DOC    Bad file data or bad password, CRC error!

ARJ      69120 95-12-28 21:05:12, DISK     69120 95-12-28 21:05:12
DATA\WINWORD\CHAP05.DOC    is same or newer, Overwrite?
Yes, No, or Quit? y
Extracting DATA\WINWORD\CHAP05.DOC    Bad file data or bad password, CRC error!

ARJ      59392 95-12-14 15:38:00, DISK     59392 95-12-14 15:38:00
DATA\WINWORD\CHAP04.DOC    is same or newer, Overwrite? y
```

CRC error resulting from incorrect password

The only thing wrong in the above example is that the password isn't capitalized. Since the password used in archiving was "Hello", the extract command fails. As with archiving commands, ARJ lets you hide password entry during extraction. Again, simply type a question mark in place of the password on the command line. For example:

```
ARJ x -g? NEWARC
```

NOTE If your files are so private that you must use password protection, consider deleting the originals once they're safely archived. The Move command does this automatically.

```
PKZIP -m -sIMPORTANT! NEWARC C:\DATA\WINWORD\*.DOC
```

Protecting SFX archives

PKZIP and ARJ support password protection for self-extracting archives. The other programs do not. It's easy to use passwords with SFX archives. For PKZIP, simply convert the protected archive, as shown below:

```
PKZIP -a -sVERY NEWARC      (first pack with scrambling password "VERY")

ZIP2EXE NEWARC      (then convert)
```

It's also easy to do this in ARJ. The command line simply includes an additional option to make the archive into a protected SFX file:

```
ARJ -a -je -gVERY NEWARC   (with password of "VERY")
```

In both examples, a self-extracting archive called "NEWARC" is built from the files in the directory and protected with the password "VERY". Use the same option ("s" or "g") again for extracting.

```
NEWARC -sVERY      (for PKZIP archive)
```

or

```
NEWARC -gVERY      (for ARJ archive)
```

The files are then unpacked as usual.

The password options are supported only by the large models of the ARJSFX and PKSFX modules. Remember that these programs also are case-sensitive.

Password protection limitations

Obviously, passwords cannot make your data completely safe from intrusion or carelessness. As we mentioned, passwords lock only the individual files within an archive instead of the archive itself. This means that the archive can still be deleted, copied, or edited with special programs.

Even the files themselves are protected only against unauthorized extraction. They can still be deleted, renamed, or overwritten from the hard drive by unprotected versions.

We'll use an example to demonstrate this problem. Suppose that a disk contains the archive NEWARC.ARJ, as shown below. You discover that all the files are garbled (a "G" appears on the right side of the listing). However, despite this protection, these files can still be accessed. For example, the following command, which deletes all archived text files, works normally without a password:

```
ARJ d NEWARC *.TXT
```

```
C:\>arj d newarc *.txt
ARJ 2.41a Copyright (c) 1990-93 Robert K Jung. Jul 10 1993
*** This SHAREWARE program is NOT REGISTERED for use in a business, commercial,
*** government, or institutional environment except for evaluation purposes.

Updating archive  : NEWARC.ARJ
Archive created: 1996-01-05 11:15:10, modified: 1996-01-05 11:39:16
Deleting DATA\WINWORD\MSFSLOG.TXT
Deleting DATA\WINWORD\README.TXT
Deleting DATA\WINWORD\NETWORK.TXT
Deleting DATA\WINWORD\PC_INFO.TXT
Deleting DATA\WINWORD\SUPPORT.TXT
     5 file(s)

C:\>
```

Deleting files in NEWARC.ARJ

The next command, which updates all the protected backup files with the extension .BAK, is also executed without any interruption from the program:

```
ARJ u NEWARC *.BAK
```

Only DOC files and BAK files remain protected since neither were affected directly by the operation.

NOTE As this example demonstrates, password protection has its limitations. Still, passwords are a good way to help keep private information safe. LHA and ZOO don't support password protection of archived files.

Comments

If you do a lot of archiving, you probably know how difficult it is to keep track of your compressed files. At the very least, you should use meaningful filenames that provide clues to the file's contents. Also, almost all compression programs are able to attach comments to entire archives or to individual compressed files. These comments provide information about the file.

When using comments, remember that they occupy disk space. However, since comments aren't compressed, you can easily determine how much they increase the storage requirement for an archive: Each character uses one additional byte.

Comments in PKZIP

In PKZIP, it's easy to add comments to archives. Two commands let you attach comments to an entire archive or to individual files. The following table shows the control parameters:

Option	Description
-z	Comment refers to archive (ZIP comment).
-c	Comment refers to an individual archived file (file comment).
-C	Used with Update or Add to attach comments only to new files being archived.

Comments can have a maximum length of 60 characters. The text of the comment isn't entered on the command line. Instead, PKZIP prompts you for the text on a separate line after you enter the command.

```
PKZIP -c SECRET
```

With the above command, you can create or edit comments for each file in an archive. If a file already has a comment, first it's displayed.

Simply type the desired comment for each file at the program prompt. If there is an old comment, your entry overwrites it. Press (Enter) to keep an existing comment and move to the next file. To delete an existing comment, type a space and then press (Enter).

```
PKZIP -c -u SECRET *.TXT
```

128

The above command updates all .TXT files in the archive called "SECRET." You are prompted for a comment for each new file that's written to the archive.

Use the **View** command to display file comments. PKZIP displays comments either in the long technical format (vt) or as an extra line on the usual columnar format (vc). Both of these formats are special options of the **View** command.

```
PKZIP -vt SECRET *.BAT
```

The above command shows, for example, all the .BAT files in the SECRET archive in long technical format. Among the information displayed for a given file is any comment currently attached to it. The columnar view, which shows several files on the same screen, is easier to read. The following command activates this format:

```
PKZIP -vc SECRET
```

Creating specific comments for each file in an archive is time-consuming. An alternative is to attach a general comment to the archive itself. An archive comment is displayed whenever the archive (ZIP file) is processed. The switch for an archive comment is "-z" (ZIP comment).

```
PKZIP -z SECRET
```

After you enter the above command, PKZIP prompts you for the archive comment. If one already exists, it's displayed before the prompt. You can revise this comment or replace it with new text. Like at the DOS level, you can copy the comment to the edit line using F3 or the → key. By doing this, you don't have to retype the text that doesn't have to be changed. The 60-character limit that applies to file comments isn't effective in this case. So, you can type up to one and a half lines before PKZIP sounds a warning beep and stops further entry. Press Enter when you're finished typing.

The program now displays the archive comment each time you work with the archive, whether you're extracting, freshening, or even simply viewing the archive contents.

Comments in ZOO

ZOO provides the same types of comment options as PKZIP but the comments can be up to 64K in length. The following commands process file or archive comments:

Option	Meaning
-c	Create or edit the file comment.
c	Same as -comment
cA	Create or edit archive comment. You must use the same capitalization when typing this command.

```
ZOO -c ARCHE *.TXT
```

The above command lets you add or revise comments for all .TXT files in the archive called "ARCHE." Any existing comments are first displayed. ZOO uses an unusual entry format here. After each comment, on a line by itself, you must type "/END" (or "/end"). So, an entry such as

```
this is my favorite archive /END
```

is interpreted as an unfinished comment that includes the /END sequence as part of its text. The correct format is the following two-line entry:

```
this is my favorite archive [Enter]
/END [Enter]
```

Now that the termination sequence is correctly placed on its own line, pressing [Enter] updates the file comment and lets you continue with the next file. Pressing [F6] and [Enter] exits the file-commentating process.

To delete an existing comment, enter the following on the first line:

```
/END
```

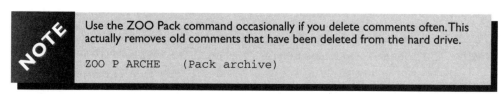

Use the ZOO Pack command occasionally if you delete comments often. This actually removes old comments that have been deleted from the hard drive.

```
ZOO P ARCHE    (Pack archive)
```

A simple addition to the comment command lets you adds comments to the archive itself:

```
ZOO cA ARCHE
```

In the above command, the added letter "A" (uppercase required) indicates an archive comment. As with file comments, an existing archive comment is displayed before you're prompted for your entry.

To display all the comments, use the **-list** command.

```
ZOO -l ARCHE
```

With the above command, each file in the archive is listed, along with any comments. Because of the large size allowed for comments, you may want to use the DOS command MORE to pause the display when the screen is full.

```
ZOO -l ARCHE | MORE
```

Add the MORE command to page through the information and read it at your own pace.

Comments in ARJ

Of all the programs, ARJ provides the largest selection of options for handling comments. Not only can you create and edit comments for both archives and their individual files, but you can also automatically apply comments that you've already created and saved in a text file. This is very helpful if, for example, you must add a general comment to several BBS archives.

```
ARJ c COPIES
```

In ARJ, the **c** command applies comments. You can move through the archive in dialog mode, editing mode, or add the comments for one file at a time. Existing comments are displayed as they are encountered.

ARJ accepts up to 25 lines of comments per file. At the prompt, enter the desired comment and press [Enter]. To keep an existing comment, press [Enter] without typing any text. To delete a comment, type a space and then press [Enter].

Instead of entering a comment from the screen, you can have ARJ read it from a text file. To do this in dialog mode, type an exclamation point followed by the filename. This is a useful way to apply long comments.

To display all the comments in an archive, use the (expanded) format. Simply add the "v" command:

```
ARJ v COPIES
```

The display is in tabular form, with each file comment immediately below its associated file entry. If you have long comments, add the "-jp" option to keep the information from scrolling off the screen before you can read it:

```
ARJ v -jp COPIES
```

When used alone, the **c** command applies to both archive and file comments. However, you can add an optional parameter on the command line to distinguish between the two types of comments.

Option	Type	Option	Type
-z	Archive comments	-jz	File comments

The ARJ program's ability to read comments from text files helps create identical comments for archives.

```
ARJ c -zLABEL.TXT COPIES
```

The above command applies a comment to the COPIES.ARJ archive. The text for the comment is taken from a file called "LABEL.TXT". The filename immediately follows the parameter. If a space is added before the filename, an error occurs. The "-z" parameter specifies that the comment should apply only to the archive itself. The individual files aren't affected. If you want to assign your own comments to the files, the command line might look as follows:

```
ARJ c COPIES -zARCHIVE.TXT -jzFILE.TXT
```

Now the comment for the COPIES archive is taken from the file called "ARCHIVE.TXT." The text from a different file, called "FILE.TXT", is applied as a comment to each of the compressed files. In this example, the parameters follow the archive name. You can also place them in front of it, as in the previous example.

It's also possible to apply a general comment to all the archives on a disk drive. This is easy to do with ARJ. First prepare the text of the comment and save it in a file. Then search the root directory and all the subdirectories and apply the prepared comment to each archive that's found.

For example, suppose that you're responsible for supplying ARJ archives to several people within your department on a regular basis. You could include the following comment:

```
Please refer problems or questions to
```

132

```
Don Michler - Ext. 5456
```

After saving the comment in a file called "REFER.TXT", you can attach it to every ARJ archive on your hard drive with a single command:

```
ARJ c -r \*.ARJ -zREFER.TXT
```

The "-r" parameter specifies that all subdirectories under the specified directory should also be processed.

By using the DOS term "NUL" instead of a filename, you can delete comments this way. The rest of the command remains the same.

```
ARJ c COPIES -zNUL
```

The above command deletes the archive comment from the COPIES archive. With the following command, all archive and file comments are deleted from all the archives on the current drive:

```
ARJ c -r \*.ARJ -zNUL -jzNUL
```

The following table summarizes the command options for handling comments in ARJ:

Option	Meaning	Option	Meaning
c	Create or edit comments in an archive.	-jzFILE -zFILE -jzNUL	Automatically attach comments found in FILE to an archive.
-z	Do archive comments only.	-zNUL	Automatically delete comments from an archive.
-jz	Do file comments only.		

Time Stamps

Your computer keeps a record for each file and directory to show the date and time when it was last updated. This is called a time stamp. To display time stamps, use the DOS command DIR.

```
D:\>dir

 Volume in drive D is D_DRIVE
 Volume Serial Number is 1F1F-7D1B
 Directory of D:\

ACCESS       <DIR>        12-20-95   8:11a ACCESS
PCINTERN     <DIR>        12-29-95  10:21a pcintern
ZIPKIT   PAS         9,517 12-20-95  12:29p zipkit.pas
ZIPKIT   BAK        12,765 12-20-95  12:23p ZIPKIT.BAK
ZIPKIT   EXE         9,968 12-20-95  12:29p ZIPKIT.EXE
GAMES        <DIR>        12-04-95   4:16a games
COMPDISK     <DIR>        12-12-95   4:09p COMPDISK
TP           <DIR>        12-13-95   4:59p TP
GDK          <DIR>        12-10-95  11:36p GDK
DPINST       <DIR>        12-10-95  11:56p DPINST
TURBO        <DIR>        12-12-95  10:06a turbo
TURBO60      <DIR>        12-12-95  10:26a TURBO60
_NO_COPY     <DIR>        12-15-95   2:46p _NO_COPY
POSTOF~1     <DIR>        12-22-95   9:27a postoffice
DOCFILES     <DIR>        01-04-96   1:29p docfiles
         3 file(s)        32,250 bytes
        12 dir(s)    192,970,752 bytes free

D:\>
```

Displaying time stamps

Time stamps are important in both compressing and uncompressing files. Except for the **Add** command, every operation that moves a file to or from an archive works with the time stamp. The **Update** and **Freshen** commands rely on this information to determine which archived files should be overwritten. For this reason, the time stamp for every file in an archive is carefully preserved, despite the extra storage space that's needed. You can observe this when you use the **View** command, for example, to display a ZIP archive.

In some compression programs, time stamps aren't limited to these functions. In addition to the **Update** and **Freshen** commands, various file selection options can be controlled by time stamps. ARJ can select files, for example, that were created either:

❖ On a certain date

❖ At a precise time on a certain date

❖ Within a certain time span

In PKZIP, you can check for files that were created or modified on or after a certain date. The option for this is "t." If a date isn't specified, the current date (today) is assumed.

```
PKZIP -urpt TODAY *.XL? *.DB? *.DOC
```

Regardless of how much work you do on your PC in a given day, you can easily update your archive with all the new or changed files by using a command like the one above. The parameters have the following meanings:

Parameter	Meaning
u	Update files.
r	Recursing all subdirectories.
p	Storing paths recursed along with filenames.
t	But only include those files that were created or modified today.

The file extensions further limit the types of files (text, Excel, and database) that will be processed.

PKZIP also lets you specify a date with the -t parameter. If you've been too busy to compress your files, just specify the date when you last did so. For example, the above command adapted for archiving files from the 20th of January, 1993, is:

```
PKZIP -arpt012093 TODAY *.DOC *.XL? *.DB?
```

The time stamp parameter can be used only in compression operations with PKZIP. It doesn't work with commands such as View, or for extracting files from an archive. The extraction program PKUNZIP uses the "-t" option to test for data corruption.

ARJ and time stamps

With ARJ, you can examine time stamps more precisely. You can specify not only a date, but also time to the nearest second. Also, there are two separate options for selecting time stamps either before or after a specified cutoff. Finally, time stamps can be used with additional commands for archive file management and extraction operations. For example, you can delete all archived files older than a certain date.

ARJ requires the date/time in descending order (from years to seconds), without separation characters. The format is as follows:

```
YYMMDDHHMMSS
```

The letters represent numeric digits in the positions shown.

YY	For the year	MM	For the month	DD	For the day

For example, January 23, 1993 at 7:07:28 pm, would appear as:

```
930123190728
```

Although this is difficult to read, you usually don't have to enter the actual time of day.

Option	Meaning
-o[YYMMDDHHMM	Selects only files created or modified on or after this date/time.
-ob[YYMMDDHHM	Selects only fileS created or modified before this date/time.

If the date/time is omitted, the current (today's) date is automatically used with both options. By using these options, you can easily find and archive your old, inactive files. Based on their time stamps, simply move the outdated ones to an archive with the **Move** command, and make room on your hard drive for more current data.

Remember that some important files are almost never updated. So, be careful when clearing old files from your hard drive because you may accidentally delete an important file. For example, using the following command to delete files, that are over a year old, from your hard drive could be disastrous:

```
ARJ m -rob920101 DEEPSIX \*.*
```

Remember, the *.* wildcard refers to both data files and program files. These files usually aren't changed after they're installed on your hard drive. So, you can destroy your operating system files by using one command. If so, your PC won't run because the command interpreter COMMAND.COM was deleted.

However, with a little care, you can limit the operation only to files that can safely be deleted. For example, most files created by application programs would fall into this category. You can identify many text files (DOC, TXT, WRI), worksheets (XL?, WK?), databases, and graphics by their extensions.

```
ARJ m -rob920101 DEEPSIX \*.DOC \*.TXT \*.WRI ...
```

The above command is much safer than the previous one. We can even improve this command further. Instead of entering all the extensions on the command line, create a list file and pass it to ARJ for processing. For example, with any text editor, you can quickly create a file called "DEEPSIX.DAT", which looks like this:

Chapter 6

```
\*.TXT
\*.DOC
\*.WRI
\*.XL?
...
```

Then you can execute the following command:

```
ARJ m -rob920101 DEEPSIX !DEEPSIX.DAT
```

The **Move** command compresses all the appropriate files to your archive and then deletes the uncompressed originals.

> Once you've deleted all the desired files, you should check the contents of the archive. This is important because you may have accidentally deleted an important file. In this case, extract it separately from the archive.

Using Attributes To Select Files

Besides a file's size and time stamp, DOS also keeps track of certain information about each file. Programs often check these file attributes and use them as the basis for decisions about file processing. The archive attribute is one of the most common attributes. Whenever a file is created or changed, DOS sets the bit for its archive attribute. This tells backup programs that the file should be archived, because it contains new or changed information. Every file has a bit for each of the attributes listed below:

	Attribute	Meaning
A	Archive	Set by DOS when a file is updated. Backup programs check this bit, then reset it after backing up the file.
H	Hidden	If set, the DIR command doesn't display the file, but it can be edited.
R	Read-only	Files with this attribute cannot be modified or deleted. If you try to do this, the DOS message, "Access denied", appears.
D	Directory	Indicates an entry is a subdirectory.
S	System	Indicates a system file, such as IO.SYS or MSDOS.SYS. System files are also hidden.

Compression programs cannot access a few of these attributes. Also, compression programs don't use all the available attributes. Taking advantage of file attribute information is important when choosing a compression program. For example, you can identify and compress empty directories by using a special attribute switch in ARJ.

Another consideration is how hidden or read-only files are processed. You'll want to know whether they can be overwritten, archived, excluded from particular types of processing, etc. All compression programs support file privacy. If the hidden or system attribute of a file is set, the file won't be compressed. You can test this yourself by changing to the root directory of your boot drive (the drive your PC starts from) and trying to compress the system files:

```
LHA  a TEST *.SYS
ARJ  a TEST *.SYS
PKZIP  TEST *.SYS
...
```

With the possible exception of HIMEM.SYS, most likely only your CONFIG.SYS file will be compressed. The system files IO.SYS and MSDOS.SYS, which both have the system attribute set, aren't included.

PKZIP and ARJ have special parameters for overriding this protection. It's important to understand the implications of file attributes, especially in archiving files. PKZIP recognizes the following attribute parameters:

PKZIP File attribute options	
-w[h,s]	Include these files in archive (The two parameters can be combined): h hidden s system
-W[h,s]	Exclude hidden (h) or system (s) files from archive. This is the default.

In ARJ, attribute parameters are handled differently:

ARJ File attribute parameters	
-a	Compresses every file, regardless of attributes.
-a1	Compresses every file (like -a) and empty directories.
-b	Compresses only updated files carrying the archive attribute (also called backup bit).
-b1	Compresses updated files (like -b) and clears the archive attribute.
-b2	Clears the archive attribute only. Is not a selection parameter.

138

The "s" and "h" options in PKZIP let you specify whether system and/or hidden files should be included in the archive.

```
PKZIP -whs ROOT C:\*.*
```

This command saves your root directory in an archive called ROOT. Even the hidden system files IO.SYS and MSDOS.SYS (IBMBIOS.COM and IBMDOS.COM in PC-DOS systems) are included. To do this in ARJ, use the "-a" parameter.

```
ARJ a -a ROOT C:\*.*
```

```
■ 80486 CPU detected.
■ XMS version 3.00 detected.
■ Novell Netware version 3.11 detected.
■ DPMI version 0.90 detected.
■ Using Normal Compression.

Creating ZIP: ROOT.ZIP
  Adding: IO.SYS        Deflating (29%), done.
  Adding: MSDOS.SYS     Deflating (85%), done.
  Adding: COMMAND.COM   Deflating (55%), done.
  Adding: DRVSPACE.BIN  Deflating (68%), done.
  Adding: AUTOEXEC.DOS  Deflating (36%), done.
  Adding: CONFIG.DOS    Deflating (22%), done.
  Adding: DETLOG.TXT    Deflating (88%), done.
  Adding: MSDOS.---     Storing  ( 0%), done.
  Adding: DETLOG.OLD    Deflating (89%), done.
  Adding: CONFIG.SYS    Deflating (22%), done.
  Adding: SCHEDULE.FIL  Storing  ( 0%), done.
  Adding: AUTOEXEC.BAT  Deflating (42%), done.
  Adding: SUHDLOG.---   Deflating (82%), done.
  Adding: SUHDLOG.DAT   Deflating (87%), done.
  Adding: BOOTLOG.TXT   Deflating (87%), done.
  Adding: DBLSPACE.BIN  Deflating (68%), done.
  Adding: SYSTEM.1ST    Deflating %16
```

Including the system and hidden files

The above figure shows that the files in question are compressed. With ARJ, you cannot distinguish between system and hidden files. However, by adding the "-a1" switch, you can save empty directories, which isn't possible in PKZIP. This makes sense only if you specify the recursion switch as well, so all subdirectories are thoroughly searched.

```
ARJ a -ra1 ALL C:\*.*
```

The above command compresses every file on the hard drive. The "-r" switch invokes subdirectory recursion, and the "-a1" ensures that protected files and empty directories will also be included.

A look at the ARJ archive after compressing with the following command reveals an unexpected result.

```
ARJ l  -a1 ROOT
```

139

The five "files" with a size of 0 bytes are obviously subdirectories. However, they are definitely not empty. The "-a1" switch cannot determine by itself whether a subdirectory is empty. Since the recursion switch was omitted, the subdirectories cannot be searched. ARJ simply archives everything for which there is an entry in the directory (and a subdirectory is simply another entry), regardless of attributes.

```
PKZIP (R)  FAST!  Create/Update Utility  Version 2.04g  02-01-93
Copr. 1989-1993 PKWARE Inc.  All Rights Reserved.  Shareware Version
PKZIP Reg. U.S. Pat. and Tm. Off.  Patent No. 5,051,745

▪ 80486 CPU detected.
▪ XMS version 3.00 detected.
▪ Novell Netware version 3.11 detected.
▪ DPMI version 0.90 detected.

Searching ZIP: ROOT.ZIP

Length  Method  Size  Ratio  Date     Time   CRC-32   Attr  Name
------  ------  ----  -----  ----     ----   ------   ----  ----
223148  DeflatN 160172 29%   07-11-95 09:50  989d1d8c shr-  IO.SYS
  1641  DeflatN    250 85%   12-21-95 15:45  b230b982 shr-  MSDOS.SYS
   158  DeflatN    124 22%   12-22-95 09:17  7c6b4185 --w-  CONFIG.SYS
129078  DeflatN  44091 66%   07-14-95 00:00  d3571d8a --w-  LOGO.SYS
 71287  DeflatN  23497 68%   07-11-95 09:50  7299249c shr-  DRVSPACE.BIN
 71287  DeflatN  23497 68%   07-11-95 09:50  7299249c shr-  DBLSPACE.BIN
   473  DeflatN    279 42%   12-21-95 15:45  23af2461 --w-  AUTOEXEC.BAT
    39  DeflatN     33 16%   01-05-96 11:54  8fc95531 --w-  GRABBER.BAT
------          ------ ---                                  --------
497111          251943 50%                                  8

C:\>
```

What has happened to the directories in the archive?

When you view archives in PKZIP and ARJ, you'll see that the attributes of the compressed files are indicated by certain symbols. The ARJ display shows these in five columns on the right. Each attribute has a letter abbreviation, as follows:

A	Archive (backup)	H	Hidden	D	Directory
S	System	R	Read-only		

PKZIP has only three columns, since the archive and directory attributes are not recognized. The attribute status of a normal file looks like this:

```
-w    AUTOEXEC.BAT
```

The "w" stands for "writeable", indicating that the file can be changed. This means that its read-only bit is switched off (as are the hidden and system bits). Other files have some of their attribute bits switched on. They might appear as:

```
shr IO.SYS
```

IO.SYS carries the system, hidden and read-only attributes.

140

Attribute masking

The term "masking" refers to setting, resetting, or checking particular bits. In the context of archiving, these bits are the file attribute bits. By clearing one or more of the hidden, system, and read-only bits, PKZIP can alter the attributes of a file as it's compressed into an archive. In normal use, PKZIP leaves the file attributes unchanged. The "-j" parameter can clear individual attribute bits. Therefore, a hidden, read-only system file can be turned into a normal writeable file.

-j[s,h,r]	Deletes the specified attribute(s) by resetting the appropriate bit(s) when used with one or more of the three letters: s System h Hidden r Read-only
If a file has none of the attributes specified, its status is unchanged.	

```
PKZIP -whs -jhrs ROOT C:\*.*
```

The above command compresses all files below the root directory into the archive called "ROOT." The "-w" parameter ensures that hidden (h) and system (s) files are also included. The "-j" option clears the packed files of all hidden (h), read-only (r), and system (s) attributes.

Data Compression Methods

The various compression programs use several data compression methods, including "squashing", "squeezing", "crunching", and "imploding." Certain methods are specifically designed for particular file or data types. Some compression programs analyze a file's content and choose a method that will produce the maximum compression.

PKZIP and ARJ are the only compression programs that actually give you a choice of methods. Although other programs may offer options for different compression algorithms, they do this only to maintain compatibility with older versions.

141

PKZIP and compression methods

PKZIP offers two compression methods and options for applying them according to file type.

Imploding	Very thorough compression. This is the default setting. Requires less memory (90K). Regardless of the option specified, this is always the method used when memory is a limiting factor.
Shrinking	Very fast Requires somewhat more memory (128K). Regardless of the option specified, this is always the method used for files under 320 bytes.

Imploding is the default method. The "-e" option lets you override the default setting with your own choice of methods.

```
-e[x,s,a,b]  Compression method options
```

Option	Meaning
-ex	All files are compressed by imploding (default).
-es	All files are compressed by shrinking.
-ea	ASCII files are compressed by imploding, binary files by shrinking.
-eb	ASCII files are compressed by shrinking, binary files by imploding.

Processing time and compressed file size vary considerably depending on the option used. The following table shows the performance figures for archiving a directory with PKZIP. These are the same files tested later with ARJ.

```
PKZIP -a -es SPEED *.*
```

Method	Time	(Cache)	Size	Compression rate
none	:21	(:16)	464,621	46.0%
-ex	:21	(:16)	464,621	46.0%
-es	:10	(:04)	574,170	56.8%
-ea	:18	(:14)	531,955	52.7%
-eb	:11	(:06)	506,836	50.2%

As you can see, there's a significant difference from ARJ. Even with exclusive use of imploding, PKZIP took only 21 seconds. The fastest method took half that time. Although the compression achieved isn't quite so good, this speed is remarkable for processing 1,010,032 bytes of data.

Although the times were further reduced by caching, the differences are much less dramatic than with ARJ. This indicates that PKZIP accesses the hard drive less than ARJ.

ARJ and data compression methods

ARJ provides the largest selection of options for data compression methods. Instead of specifying a particular algorithm, you indicate the relative importance of speed versus packing density. According to the ARJ documentation, every improvement in speed is obtained only by sacrificing density. The switch for faster compression is "-m" and a number from 1 to 4.

Option	Meaning	Option	Meaning
-m1	Maximum (highest density) compression.	-m3	Faster still, but with less compression.
-m2	Somewhat less compression, slightly faster.	-m4	Maximum speed.

In addition to the "-m" switch, there is another option for optimizing compression density with m1 and m2.

Option	Meaning
-jm1	Maximum (highest density) compression (improvement of m1).
-jm2	Improvement of m2.

The -j optimizing switch should be used with m1 and m2 only. The results are uncertain when -j is used with m3 or m4,

You're probably wondering whether having such precise control over packing density and speed is really useful. Usually differences in the results of the various options are small. For testing purposes, we built a directory consisting of Word documents, ASCII files, and binary files in equal proportions. Then we archived the directory using each of the ARJ compression modes. The following table shows some surprising results:

```
ARJ a -jm MAX *.*
```

Method	Time	(Cache)	Size	Compression rate
-jm1	1:14	(0:17)	436,051	43.2%
-jm2	1:12	(0:16)	436,568	43.2%
-m1	1:13	(0:11)	436,573	43.2%
-m2	1:11	(0:08)	440,346	43.6%
-m3	1:07	(0:18)	450,985	44.6%
-m4	1:10	(0:17)	496,031	49.1%

Methods m1 to m4 are not radically different in terms of time or compression. All compression rates remain under 50%, which is fairly good for mixed data with a high proportion of binary files. m4, the fastest algorithm, is only four seconds faster than the slowest. An extra 60K of memory was required for this gain in speed.

❖ The m0 method archives files without any compression.

❖ The ARJ SFX module does not support the m4 method.

❖ The jm3 and jm4 methods are undefined and lead to unpredictable results.

Use a memory cache to speed up hard drive access during data compression. Doing this can save a significant amount of time, as shown by method m2. The entire compression process was shortened from 1 minute 11 seconds to just 8 seconds.

However, this is only possible because ARJ accesses the hard drive so intensively. Since PKZIP does less disk accessing, it can perform much faster. However, using a cache doesn't improve PKZIP's performance. This is shown in a table later in this section.

An archive listing shows the compression method that was used for each file:

```
■ 80486 CPU detected.
■ XMS version 3.00 detected.
■ Novell Netware version 3.11 detected.
■ DPMI version 0.90 detected.

Searching ZIP: TEST.ZIP

Length  Method   Size  Ratio   Date     Time   CRC-32    Attr  Name
------  ------   ----  -----   ----     ----   ------    ----  ----
 72192  DeflatN  20175  73%  12-14-95  16:29  b544d017  --w-  CHAP03.DOC
 44544  DeflatN  15463  66%  12-14-95  14:46  1ba09ce2  --w-  CHAP01.DOC
 38400  DeflatN  10231  74%  12-15-95  09:38  6438ae19  --w-  CHAP02.DOC
 15954  DeflatN   5250  68%  07-11-95  09:50  e29c98b2  --w-  DISPLAY.DOC
  7072  DeflatN   2610  64%  07-11-95  09:50  c6acf3cf  --w-  EXCHANGE.DOC
 17752  DeflatN   5475  70%  07-11-95  09:50  39065bf8  --w-  CONFIG.DOC
  1356  DeflatS    323  77%  01-03-96  12:35  037d8715  --w-  MSFSLOG.TXT
  7302  DeflatS   2606  65%  12-18-95  10:16  bacdf1a8  --w-  README.TXT
 18538  DeflatS   7189  62%  07-11-95  09:50  bb9922f6  --w-  NETWORK.TXT
  7036  DeflatS   3149  56%  12-11-95  16:05  566b9939  --w-  PC_INFO.TXT
  6823  DeflatS   2823  59%  07-11-95  09:50  81192770  --w-  SUPPORT.TXT
------          ------  ---                                   -------
236969           75294  69%                                   11

C:\>
```

Compression method shown in the method

The M-column on the right side of the display indicates the compression method the program used to compress the file. If this seems complicated, don't worry. ARJ automatically recognizes the compression method used and chooses the appropriate extraction method accordingly.

While using ARJ, we didn't place any restrictions on archiving time or memory requirements. The standard m1 setting was sufficient.

If you're concerned about these considerations, you should be aware of the memory requirements listed in the following table. These requirements are associated with the different compression methods.

ARJ Memory Requirement			
Method	Requirement	Method	Requirement
-m1	at least 300K	-m3	at least 250K
-m2	at least 282K	-m4	at least 235K

Using PKZIP As a Multi-packer

There used to be only one way to transfer large quantities of data between computers. First, you had to store the desired files from the source computer on several diskettes by using the DOS BACKUP command. Next, the contents of the diskettes had to be placed on the target computer's hard drive by using the RESTORE command. Problems could occur if both computers had different versions of DOS. For example, a system running DOS 2.1 couldn't RESTORE an archive created by the BACKUP command of DOS 3.3.

Let's say you have several files you've created that you want to compress into one convenient "zipped" file. You zip the file or files just as you normally would do. But, after you've zipped your files you notice it's over 2 Meg in size and your diskettes only hold 1.4 Meg. Obviously in won't fit on one diskette. You have a problem. But there is a simple solution.

PKZIP has a powerful, yet often misunderstood feature that let's you "link" or "span" more than one diskette with one zipped file larger than 1 or more diskettes (or more precisely, create zipped files of almost unlimited size). With the right commands, you can 'span' several diskettes until PKZIP has completed its compression.)

Before we show you how to do this you will need one or more formatted diskettes. If you do not, consult your DOS manual for the directions on how to format diskettes. Be sure to label your blank, formatted diskettes. For example, disk 1, disk 2, etc. It'll save you and anyone unzipping the files time and effort later. (A quick note; for the more adventuresome we have included a few advanced examples of creating large zipped files on unformatted diskettes at the end of this chapter.

Here's how you create a large zipped file that will link (or span) two (or more) formatted diskettes.

At the DOS prompt type:

```
pkzip a:\test.zip *.* -&
```

and press Enter

The important keys to this procedure is that we use the drive letter A (our 3 1/2" disk drive) as part of the zipped file name and the 'switch' (or command) '-&'. If you are interested in learning more about these options be sure to consult the MANUAL.DOC of PKZIP. And remember. After you have created your large zipped file that fills several diskettes, label them. This will save you or someone else time and effort when uncompressing this file.

Uncompressing a zipped file of several diskettes

When you insert the diskette that you labeled the first disk (usually #1) type the following to begin unzipping this file:

```
PKUNZIP A:\ZIPFILE.ZIP
```

and press (Enter).

```
C:\>pkunzip a:\zipfile.zip

PKUNZIP (R)    FAST!    Extract Utility    Version 2.04e  01-25-93
Copr. 1989-1993 PKWARE Inc. All Rights Reserved. Shareware Version
PKUNZIP Reg. U.S. Pat. and Tm. Off.

■ 80486 CPU detected.
■ XMS version 3.00 detected.

Searching ZIP: A:/ZIPFILE.ZIP
Insert the LAST disk of the backup set - Press a key when ready
```

PKUNZIP will prompt for the last disk to be inserted. This is to check the zipped file. PKUNZIP will then look at this diskette and ask you to reinsert disk #1. PKUNZIP will then unzip each diskette and ask for each subsequent diskette until the file is uncompressed.

Using ARJ As A Multi-packer

When an archive must span multiple diskettes, ARJ effortlessly performs the necessary management for you. You don't have to worry about file sizes, disk space, or what goes where.

The "-v" switch lets an archive span more than one volume. Several other options provide added flexibility and power to the multi-volume archiving process. Used with every possible option, the "-v" switch looks like this:

```
-vvwa360sCOMMAND
```

The following table should clarify this command line:

Option	Meaning
-v	Creates a multi-volume archive.
v	Sounds a beep between volumes.
w	Prevents archived files from being split across volumes.
360	Specifies maximum volume size in bytes. Units of 1000 (not 1024) can be abbreviated as K.
a	Checks space available on target medium before starting a new volume.
s	Executes a command or batch file before starting a new target volume. Spaces between the 's' and the command or filename aren't permitted.

Creating a simple multi-volume archive

Despite the confusing array of parameter options, creating a multi-volume archive is easy. For example, if you want to archive all files in the current directory to diskettes, simply type:

```
ARJ a -va A:TRANSFER
```

The "-v" switch ensures that the archiving process isn't aborted if the diskette in drive A: becomes full. The "-v" alone, however, isn't sufficient. ARJ must know how large the individual archive volumes can be. Maximum volume size is controlled by the "a" option, as used above, or by specifying a size directly.

148

When a divided archive requires another diskette, ARJ prompts you to insert one in the target drive.

After inserting the new diskette, simply enter "Yes" to continue compressing. ARJ checks to see that there is free space on the diskette. If there isn't, you can switch diskettes and enter "Yes" again. The "v" option tells ARJ to prompt you with a beep when it's time to change diskettes.

```
ARJ a -vva A:TRANSFER
```

ARJ beeps before starting a new archive volume.

Unlike most of the other switches, the "-v" switch requires that options be entered in a specific order. To activate the warning beep, you must place the "v" option directly after the "-v" switch:

This is correct:

```
ARJ a -vv HELLO
```

This is incorrect:

```
ARJ a -vav HELLO
```

The "a" switch specifies that ARJ should automatically determine the maximum volume size. Before starting to write a new volume, the program checks to see how much free space is on the target storage medium (ARJ doesn't overwrite existing data). The available free space becomes the maximum size for that volume.

If you use the "a" switch with other options, remember to place it on the command line correctly (after "v" and "w").

The following is an example:

```
ARJ a -vvwa b:HELLO
```

You can divide an archive into multiple volumes even on your hard drive. In this case, the "a" switch isn't appropriate, since you want to restrict the volume size to less than the available free space. To do this, you can specify the size limit directly, as in the following examples:

```
ARJ a -v360000 B:\TRANS -wC:\
```

or

```
ARJ a -v360K B:\TRANS -wC:\
```

The above command creates a multi-volume archive called "TRANS" on drive B:. Regardless of the type of diskette you insert in the drive, the size of a single volume is limited to 360,000 bytes. (To save time, a temporary archive is also created on the C: drive.) The only difference between the second command and the first is that thousands are expressed as K. Remember that, in this instance, K means 1,000 instead of 1,024.

If the specified amount of storage isn't available, ARJ warns you before starting the new volume.

```
C:\>arj a -v360 -R A:HELLO C:\*.TXT *.DOC *.BAT
ARJ 2.41a Copyright (c) 1990-93 Robert K Jung. Jul 10 1993
*** This SHAREWARE program is NOT REGISTERED for use in a business, commercial
*** government, or institutional environment except for evaluation purposes.

A:HELLO.ARJ
Warning! Only 23552 bytes of free disk space. Continue?
```

You can respond to the warning with the usual "Yes", "No", "All", or "Quit" ARJ commands. ARJ recognizes size abbreviations for the four popular diskette formats. For example, instead of "362000", you can simply use "360".

Abbreviation	Meaning	Abbreviation	Meaning
360	362,000 bytes	1200	1,213,000 bytes
720	730,000 bytes	1440	1,457,000 bytes

```
ARJ a -v360 A:HELLO

ARJ a -v1440 D:TRANS
```

The first example creates a multi-volume archive named "HELLO" on the A: drive. Volume size is limited to 360K. The second command creates an archive named "TRANS" on the D: drive, whose volumes are each limited to 1440K.

Each volume of a divided archive needs a unique name. ARJ uses the normal extension ARJ for the first volume, then assigns ascending numbers after the letter "A" to subsequent volumes. For example, the command:

```
ARJ a -v10000 PARTS \*.TXT *.BAT
```

might create the following volumes:

```
Volume in drive C is C_DRIVE
Volume Serial Number is 201A-1EE9
Directory of C:\test

             <DIR>       01-08-96   9:53a  .
             <DIR>       01-08-96   9:53a  ..
HELLO    000        19,394   01-08-96   9:52a  HELLO.000
HELLO    001        19,416   01-08-96   9:52a  HELLO.001
HELLO    002        19,400   01-08-96   9:52a  HELLO.002
HELLO    003        19,400   01-08-96   9:52a  HELLO.003
HELLO    004        19,400   01-08-96   9:52a  HELLO.004
HELLO    005        19,400   01-08-96   9:52a  HELLO.005
HELLO    006        19,400   01-08-96   9:52a  HELLO.006
HELLO    007        19,400   01-08-96   9:52a  HELLO.007
HELLO    008        19,400   01-08-96   9:52a  HELLO.008
HELLO    009        19,400   01-08-96   9:52a  HELLO.009
HELLO    010        19,400   01-08-96   9:52a  HELLO.010
HELLO    011        19,400   01-08-96   9:52a  HELLO.011
HELLO    012        19,400   01-08-96   9:52a  HELLO.012
HELLO    013        19,400   01-08-96   9:52a  HELLO.013
HELLO    014        19,400   01-08-96   9:52a  HELLO.014
       15 file(s)         291,010 bytes
        2 dir(s)      492,011,520 bytes free

C:\test>
```

Naming archive volumes

File extensions for all but the first volume start with A01 and go through A00. This limits the normal number of volumes in a single archive to 101. It sounds like a generous limit, but even this can be overridden. To allow for as many as 1,000 volumes (this should be sufficient), specify the file extension .000 (or you could start with some other number, such as 00, allowing for a lesser total). The command would look like this:

```
ARJ a -v20K PLENTY.000
```

ARJ will name the first volume with the extension you specify and number subsequent ones sequentially. The last possible volume would have the extension .999. However, if necessary, the volume size can still be increased.

Optimizing memory space

In filling archive volumes, ARJ tries to use the available space as completely as possible. This may involve splitting a file that cannot fit at the end of a volume and continuing it at the beginning of the next. With this technique of space optimization, the program can come within 200 bytes of the maximum volume size. You can prevent ARJ from splitting files by adding the "w" switch to the command line. Remember, this option must be placed after the "v" (prompt with beep) and before the "a" (automatic volume size) or specified volume size.

```
ARJ a -vwav ...  ( wrong )
ARJ a -vvwa ...  ( right )
ARJ a -vw360 ... ( right )
```

When files cannot be split, more space is wasted. To demonstrate this, we'll compare two commands. The only difference between these commands is the "w" option. Both operations compress the text files *.TXT to a 50,000 byte per volume multi-volume archive on the hard drive. The optimized archive is called "OPT_Y" and is created with the following command:

```
ARJ a -r -v50K OPT_Y \*.TXT
```

The nonoptimized archive is called "OPT_N" and is created with the following command:

```
ARJ a -r -vw50K OPT_N \*.TXT
```

The effect of optimization is apparent in a DIR listing:

```
C:\test>DIR OPT_Y

 Volume in drive C is C_DRIVE
 Volume Serial Number is 201A-1EE9
 Directory of C:\test

OPT_Y    ARJ      49,240  01-08-96  10:31a OPT_Y.ARJ
OPT_Y    A01      49,326  01-08-96  10:31a OPT_Y.A01
OPT_Y    A02      49,358  01-08-96  10:31a OPT_Y.A02
OPT_Y    A03      49,295  01-08-96  10:31a OPT_Y.A03
OPT_Y    A04      49,319  01-08-96  10:31a OPT_Y.A04
OPT_Y    A05      49,275  01-08-96  10:31a OPT_Y.A05
OPT_Y    A06      49,375  01-08-96  10:31a OPT_Y.A06
OPT_Y    A07      49,323  01-08-96  10:31a OPT_Y.A07
OPT_Y    A08      49,362  01-08-96  10:31a OPT_Y.A08
OPT_Y    A09      21,166  01-08-96  10:31a OPT_Y.A09
        10 file(s)         465,039 bytes
         0 dir(s)      489,062,400 bytes free

C:\test>
```

The listing of the OPT_N archive shows the difference:

```
C:\test>DIR OPT_N

 Volume in drive C is C_DRIVE
 Volume Serial Number is 201A-1EE9
 Directory of C:\test

OPT_N    ARJ      44,786  01-08-96 10:31a OPT_N.ARJ
OPT_N    A01      46,364  01-08-96 10:32a OPT_N.A01
OPT_N    A02      49,255  01-08-96 10:32a OPT_N.A02
OPT_N    A03      45,960  01-08-96 10:32a OPT_N.A03
OPT_N    A04      48,735  01-08-96 10:32a OPT_N.A04
OPT_N    A05      48,353  01-08-96 10:32a OPT_N.A05
OPT_N    A06      48,922  01-08-96 10:32a OPT_N.A06
OPT_N    A07      46,373  01-08-96 10:32a OPT_N.A07
OPT_N    A08      47,503  01-08-96 10:32a OPT_N.A08
OPT_N    A09      33,127  01-08-96 10:32a OPT_N.A09
        10 file(s)          459,378 bytes
         0 dir(s)       489,029,632 bytes free

C:\test>
```

It's obvious that the nonoptimized archive has more volumes. Now let's compare the average volume size. Not counting the last (partial) volume in each archive, we arrive at the following figures:

Archive	Average size	Archive	Average size
OPT_Y	46,186 bytes	OPT_N	45,764 bytes

As you can see, not using space on diskettes efficiently is a serious problem. Therefore, allowing files to be split by omitting the "w" switch can save both time and diskettes.

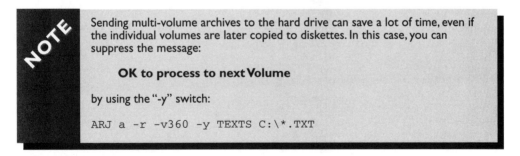

NOTE

Sending multi-volume archives to the hard drive can save a lot of time, even if the individual volumes are later copied to diskettes. In this case, you can suppress the message:

OK to process to next Volume

by using the "-y" switch:

```
ARJ a -r -v360 -y TEXTS C:\*.TXT
```

Combining commands

Now let's return to the task we discussed at the beginning of this section. All the files in a directory must be archived to diskettes (assuming more than one is needed) on the A: drive.

```
ARJ a -va A:TRANSFER
```

Each time a diskette on the target drive is full, ARJ prompts you to insert another diskette and indicate that you're ready to continue. If the new diskette doesn't have enough free space, the following warning message appears:

```
C:\>ARJ A -VA -Y A:TRANSFER
ARJ 2.41a Copyright (c) 1990-93 Robert K Jung. Jul 10 1993
*** This SHAREWARE program is NOT REGISTERED for use in a business, commercial,
*** government, or institutional environment except for evaluation purposes.

A:TRANSFER.ARJ

Not enough free disk space!


C:\>
```

At this point, you cannot delete files or format the diskette. So, you must have a sufficient supply of formatted blank diskettes ready before executing the above command.

It's also possible to alter the ARJ command by attaching a DOS command to it. Before ARJ starts a new volume, the DOS command will be executed. This gives you a chance to interrupt ARJ and format the diskette or delete files. The "s" switch is used for attaching the command. This option immediately follows the command, without being separated by a space. ARJ accepts the following:

❖ Internal DOS commands (e.g., DIR)

❖ Programs (e.g., FORMAT, COMMAND)

❖ Batch files

Batch files can be used to automate all the necessary steps for dealing with diskettes and the hard drive. The "s" switch must be placed after all others.

```
ARJ a -vvwasCOMMAND.COM A:SAVE
```

The above command is an excellent example for creating a multi-volume archive, using all the available options in the correct sequence. The "s" switch ensures that the command interpreter COMMAND.COM runs before ARJ begins each volume of the SAVE archive, including the first. So, when you execute the command, you'll see the following DOS message first instead of the usual filename and percent display (assuming that you're using DOS 6.20):

```
C:\>command

Microsoft(R) MS-DOS(R) Version 6.20
            (C)Copyright Microsoft Corp 1981-1993.

C:\>
```

This takes you a level higher in the operating environment and places ARJ in the background. The diskette can be processed as required, using DIR, FORMAT, DELETE, etc. The only thing that could cause problems is calling ARJ again.

You'll return to ARJ automatically, once you've finished the necessary disk management tasks, by simply leaving COMMAND.COM with the EXIT command.

```
EXIT
```

ARJ now proceeds as normal. COMMAND.COM is called again when a new volume must be started. The process is then repeated.

Be careful when using a command that contains a space. For example, the following command:

```
ARJ a -vsDIR A:\ A:HMMM
```

will cause problems, because ARJ will interpret the archive name as "A:\" (an invalid construction), instead of the intended "HMMM on drive A:." The solution is simple. Enclose the entire multi-volume parameter string, beginning with "-v", in quotes:

```
ARJ a "-vsDIR A:\ " A:HMMM
```

Notice that we've deliberately left a space between the backslash and the closing quote. If we didn't do this, ARJ would interpret the quote as part of the path because the program expects the path to be terminated by a space. So, remember when specifying a path, put a space before the closing quote.

Using batch files to check files

Batch files can make the archiving process even easier. The following tasks in the multi-volume archiving process could be automated by using a batch file:

❖ Determine whether a diskette has data on it.

❖ If it does, delete the data from the diskette.

Only a simple DIR command is needed to check a diskette for existing files. Deleting files is slightly more complicated. The batch file can indicate whether the diskette contains data but you must decide whether the data should be deleted. Also, a batch file cannot accept and interpret your instructions without some help.

First, a routine, which accepts input from the keyboard, is needed. To do this, you'll need the DOS program DEBUG and a small text file you can create yourself. Let's call this file "KEYS.DEB." Copy the coding for the text file exactly from the following lines:

```
a 100
MOV AH,07
INT 21
MOV AH,4C
INT 21

r cx
8
n KEYS.COM
w
q
```

The KEYS.DEB text file now contains the commands that should be passed to the DOS debugger to create a program called KEYS.COM. To do this, type the following:

```
DEBUG<KEYS.DEB
```

If an error doesn't occur, KEYS.COM is now ready. However, when you call the program with

```
KEYS
```

there is no apparent response. However, when you type any character, you return to normal processing. This occurs because KEYS simply waits for a character from the keyboard. When it receives one, it checks it and saves it in the DOS variable called ERRORLEVEL. Now a batch file can see which key was pressed and take an appropriate action.

Let's look at a batch file called DISKTEST.BAT that can perform these tasks. First it provides a directory listing for the selected drive, then reacts to a YES/NO user response to delete any files.

```
@ECHO OFF
  REM
  REM     DISKTEST.BAT
  REM     Makes sure a diskette is ready
  REM     for multi-volume archiving.

  ECHO.
  If %1x==A:x Goto Continue
  If %1x==B:x Goto Continue
  If %1x==a:x Goto Continue
  If %1x==b:x Goto Continue

  ECHO No diskette drive was given (A: or B:).
  ECHO.
  Goto End

:Continue
  DIR %1 /p
  ECHO.
  PAUSE
  ECHO.
  ECHO Should diskette in %1 be erased ???
  ECHO Please enter (y)es or (n)o.
  ECHO.

  KEYS
```

```
 IF  ERRORLEVEL  121  GOTO  Delete
 IF  ERRORLEVEL  110  GOTO  End
 IF  ERRORLEVEL  89   GOTO  Delete
 IF  ERRORLEVEL  78   GOTO  End
 GOTO  End

:Delete
 ECHO  y  |  DEL  %1\*.*
 ECHO.

:End
 Echo  Press  any  key
 Echo  to  return  to  ARJ.
 Echo.
 Pause>NUL
```

To use DISKTEST.BAT with ARJ, simply type:

```
ARJ  a  "-vvasDISKTEST A:  "  A:OK
```

Before starting a new volume of the OK archive on drive A:, ARJ runs the DISKTEST program. This in turn ensures that the diskette on the indicated drive is ready for writing. If the DISKTEST drive parameter is omitted, the diskette isn't checked.

Extracting multi-volume archives

Extracting multi-volume archives is even easier than creating them. Simply type the "-v" switch to tell ARJ that the archive is divided. Any of the special options used in creating the archive can be omitted from the extraction command.

```
ARJ  x  -v  B:LONG
```

This command extracts a multi-volume archive beginning with the volume called LONG.ARJ. The numbering of the file extensions for subsequent volumes makes it possible for ARJ to restore all files and directories in an orderly sequence. If you assigned your own extensions instead of using the default naming scheme when you archived your text file, you must provide the full name of the first volume when extracting:

```
ARJ  x  -vv  B:LONG.A01
```

or

```
ARJ  x  -vv  LONGER.000
```

158

If you extract or otherwise process a divided archive without the "-v" switch, the volume specified will be handled as normal, but processing will not continue to subsequent volumes. For example, the following command extracts the first volume, but ignores the remaining 999:

```
ARJ x B:LONG.000
```

It's easy to access a particular file or group of files in a divided archive. For example, to extract all text files (TXT or DOC) from the multi-volume TEXTS archive, use the command:

```
ARJ x -v TEXTS *.DOC *.TXT
```

The only difference between this and the usual extracting command is the "-v" switch, which ensures that all volumes will be searched for the specified files.

If the "-v" is omitted in this example, only the first volume will be searched.

Listing multi-volume archives

The **List** and **View** commands can also be applied to multi-volume archives. Again, it's important to include the "-v" switch if you want to display all the volumes.

```
ARJ l -v TEXTS
```

Beginning with TEXTS.ARJ, the program lists all volumes of the TEXTS archive. The screen pauses so you can change diskettes.

The View command can also be used with archives created on multiple disks with PKZIP. Insert the last disk and type the following:

```
PKZIP -v a:\ZIPFILE.ZIP
```

Make certain to insert the last disk. Your results should be similar to the following illustration:

```
C:\>pkzip -v a:\zipfile.zip

PKZIP (R)    FAST!    Create/Update Utility    Version 2.04e    01-25-93
Copr. 1989-1993 PKWARE Inc.  All Rights Reserved.  Shareware Version
PKZIP Reg. U.S. Pat. and Tm. Off.    Patent No. 5,051,745

■ 80486 CPU detected.
■ XMS version 3.00 detected.
■ Novell Netware version 3.11 detected.

Searching ZIP: A:/ZIPFILE.ZIP

 Length  Method    Size  Ratio    Date      Time    CRC-32  Attr  Name
 ------  ------    ----  -----    ----      ----    ------  ----  ----
 291262  DeflatN   81331  73%   01-08-96   12:48   28815b8b  --w-  SAMPLE.TXT
1278248  DeflatN 1012513  21%   08-02-95   16:29   889c18c7  --w-  SAMPLE.PCX
 309696  DeflatN  141387  55%   09-30-93   06:20   604bf3de  --w-  SAMPLE.EXE
 860970  DeflatN  139403  84%   02-01-95   00:00   27cbc48f  --w-  SAMPLE.DBF
1282062  DeflatN  781419  40%   01-08-96   13:50   0cb808c3  --w-  SAMPLE.BMP
 ------          -------  ---                                      -------
4022238          2156053  47%                                           5

C:\>
```

An example of using PKZIP to view 2 or more disks

160

EXE Compressors

How EXE Compressors Work

Data compression is a complex subject. Many techniques have been developed for compressing programs into executable archives. Authors of advanced program-compression products must thoroughly understand compression schemes, the inner workings of the operating system, and program file structures.

Certain file types are indicated by their filename extensions. For

The most important advantage of file compression is saving disk space. However, compressed data must be restored to its original format before you can use it. This causes problems for many of today's programs. Although programs cannot run until they are decompressed, the decompression process itself requires space and time.

Fabric Bellard developed an alternative to the conventional concepts of data compression. In his system, a program resides in compressed form on the disk and is decompressed directly into memory when it's executed. His program, called LZEXE, quickly became popular.

Other shareware programmers have developed programs using the Bellard system. We'll discuss three programs in this chapter: LZEXE, PKLite and DIET.

example, COM and EXE are program extensions. Each indicates certain criteria according to the way the program is structured. A process that decompresses a program into memory must consider the program's structure carefully; otherwise problems will occur. The main differences between COM and EXE files are program size and the way the program code is constructed.

As we mentioned, the program resides in compressed form on the disk and must be decompressed into memory for execution. Similar to a self-extracting (SFX) archive, the EXE archive containing the compressed program also contains a small module that performs the extraction process. Its final action, once the executable code has been loaded into memory, is to start it running.

Since the compressed version still remains on the disk, there is no need to recompress the program after using it. The executable version in RAM can simply be deleted.

COM and EXE file structures

COM files are a simpler and more compact type of program than EXE files. The COM format is based on the old CP/M (the standard operating system before MS-DOS). It's characterized by its maximum program size of 64K. The 64K barrier is a characteristic of the 80x86 processor.

A computer's total memory area is divided into of 64K segments. You can imagine this as a street with a million people living along it. Instead of each person having a separate house with a separate address (such as, 5 RAM St.), the people are crowded into high-rise apartment buildings. So, a person's address could be 1,267 RAM St., Apt. 45,600.

The COM program, however, is confined to a single segment. All its data and instructions are referenced relative to the beginning of the segment, in which the program is loaded. This makes it easy to determine addresses. "House numbers" (segment addresses) aren't needed. In a COM program, you need only the "apartment number" to locate the desired "resident." Because of this, it's also easy to work with compressed COM files.

EXE programs are more difficult for compressors to manipulate, because the 64K limit does not apply to them. Therefore, EXE programs can be as large as the available memory. They can even be larger than the available memory if overlays are used. Overlays are sections of a program that can be moved in and out of memory as needed.

Segment boundaries aren't an obstacle for EXE programs. To return to our high-rise apartment building example, a complete address would now consist of both a house number and an apartment number. In other words, besides the relative location within a segment, we must specify the segment itself. However, since we can never be sure just where in RAM a program is loaded, the segment addresses used in an EXE program must be calculated at run time.

This makes it very difficult to extract an EXE file directly into memory.

Limitations of program compressors

Although they are powerful, program compressors still have their limitations. These compressors especially have problems with certain EXE models.

Programs written for MS-Windows belong to this problem category. Their EXE format differs from that of "normal" EXE files written for DOS. Windows programs contain a lot of information that isn't part of the classical model assumed by the EXE compressors.

To use memory effectively, by swapping program sections in and out, an EXE file uses overlays. EXE compressors can handle normal overlays. However, if overlays must be linked at specified memory locations, EXE compression probably won't work.

Some programs (e.g., Turbo Pascal) modify themselves. Instead of being written to an external file, which usually occurs, configuration data can be placed at a specified location directly within the EXE file. This isn't compatible with the concept of compression, where the executable code resides only temporarily in memory.

The last group of problem programs are ones that perform a self-test before starting, such as Microsoft's debugger, CODEVIEW.EXE. Each time it executes, CODEVIEW checks to see whether the program has been changed. The manipulations performed by an EXE compressor will be detected, and the program won't continue.

Using EXE compressors

The program compressors are much easier to use than normal archiving programs, because almost no optional parameters are needed. Except in DIET, which is actually more than a program compressor, the **Run** command is reduced to a simple program conversion request, similar to the following:

```
LZEXE program
```

```
PKLITE program
```

In the following sections, we'll discuss the various EXE compressors in more detail.

LZEXE

The classic program compressor is LZEXE. The French author Fabrice Ballard made this special-purpose compression program available to PC users by releasing it as shareware. We'll discuss Version 0.91. LZEXE was originally written in French but some English-language versions exist. The English help screen is as follows:

```
C:\>lzexe
LZEXE.EXE  Ver 0.91 (ENG) (c) 1989 Fabrice BELLARD
High Performance Executable File Compactor

Syntax: LZEXE «filename» [.EXE]
«filename» is the name of the .EXE file you wish to compact
The [.EXE] file extention may be omitted.
The output file will be written to the current directory

For more information, please read LZEXE.DOC [.ENG]

  ┌────────────────────────────────────────────────────────────┐
  │ This program was concieved and designed by Fabrice BELLARD who │
  │ graciously decided to submit this version into FREEWARE.     │
  │ If you have any problems or any suggestions about this program, │
  │ please write to:            Fabrice BELLARD               │
  │                        451 chemin du mas de matour         │
  │                           34790 GRABELS    (FRANCE)        │
  │                                                             │
  │ or send a message in BAL on RTEL or QBSS under the name: FAB │
  └────────────────────────────────────────────────────────────┘

C:\>
```

LZEXE help screen

The syntax of LZEXE is:

```
LZEXE <<filename>>.[.EXE]
```

The only parameter that's needed is the program name of the EXE file to be compressed.

```
LZEXE ARJ
```

The above command tells LZEXE to compress the program PKUNZIP.EXE.

```
C:\>LZEXE ARJ
LZEXE.EXE  Ver 0.91 (ENG) (c) 1989 Fabrice BELLARD
High Performance Executable File Compactor

Compacting »» ARJ.EXE
Reading the Header
Reading the Relocation Table
Compacting the .EXE File - This may take time
Writing the De-Compactor
Writing the Compacted Relocation Table
Updating the Header

Compactor Finished

Compressed 115808 > 84409 bytes
Gain: 31399 bytes   (27.11%)

Renaming » ARJ.EXE to ARJ.OLD
 & LZEXE.TMP to ARJ.EXE

C:\>
```

LZEXE work report

The following happened:

164

❖ The (original) ARJ.EXE file was renamed "ARJ.OLD".

❖ The new ARJ.EXE file was successfully compressed.

You can try it out right away. Start the compressed EXE version as you normally would:

```
ARJ
```

Without any noticeable delay, ARJ should start.

Windows programs and LZEXE

Although the LZEXE documentation warned against it, we tried to compress a Windows program called CALC.EXE.

```
LZEXE CALC
```

The attempt failed although the compression rate looked amazing at first:

CALC.EXE	811	CACL.OLD	59392

If you think this looks too good to be true, you're right. We got an error when we tried to start the program under Windows, which "proves" what we already know: Windows programs should not be compressed with LZEXE.

```
C:\>lzexe calc
LZEXE.EXE  Ver 0.91 (ENG) (c) 1989 Fabrice BELLARD
High Performance Executable File Compactor

Compacting >>> CALC.EXE
Reading the Header

The Source file calls external overlays (read LZEXE.DOC)
File size is now 59392 bytes even though it should be only  1168 bytes
This could pose problems with the execution of the compacted program,
but if the size difference is not too great, you may attempt the compact
anyway
Abort program? (O=Yes)(O/N):
```

An error occurs with Windows programs

Compressing COM files

LZEXE cannot handle COM files. So, these files must be converted to EXE files before they are compressed with LZEXE. The accessory program COMTOEXE is used for this purpose. COMTOEXE is easy to use. For example, suppose that you want to compress the DOS program MODE.COM. Use the following commands:

```
COMTOEXE MODE.COM
LZEXE MODE
```

These commands had the following effect on memory space:

MODE.COM	29,191	MODE.OLD	29,223	MODE.EXE	16,363

Once you've determined that the procedure was successful, you should delete MODE.COM and MODE.OLD to reap the benefits of the compression.

PKLite

The same company producing PKZIP/UNZIP also makes PKLite. Like PKZIP, PKLite displays a help screen, which can be called without any parameters.

```
PKLITE (tm)   Executable File Compressor   Version 1.03   12-20-90
Copyright 1990 PKWARE Inc.  All Rights Reserved.

Usage: PKLITE [options] [d:][/path]Infile [[d:][/path]Outfile]
Options are:
  -a = always compress files with overlays
  -b = make backup .BAK file of original
  -e = make compressed file unextractable (* commercial version only *)
  -l = display software license screen
  -n = never compress files with overlays
  -o = overwrite output file if it exists
  -r = remove overlay data
  -u = update file time/date to current time/date
  -x = expand a compressed file

(*) See documentation and license screen for more information

If you find PKLITE easy, and convenient to use, a registration of $46.00
would be appreciated.  Registration includes one free upgrade to the
software and a printed manual.  Please state the version of the software
that you currently have.  Send check or money order to:
                PKWARE, Inc.
                7545 N. Port Washington Rd.
                Glendale, WI 53217
C:\>
```

PKLite help screen

As you can see, you can control PKLite's options by using special parameters.

166

Compressing programs

In its simplest application, without any options, PKLite is as easy to use as LZEXE. In fact, it's actually easier because COM programs can be compressed directly, without converting them first.

Although PKLite doesn't provide a lot of information, it does indicate which files were reduced, from what size, to what size. It doesn't distinguish between COM and EXE files. The compressed version overwrites the original file.

If you want to save the original, add a different name for the compressed version to your command.

```
PKLITE MODE.COM CMODE.COM
```

In the above example, the new file is named "CMODE.COM." If the new file already exists, PKLITE asks if you want to overwrite it.

Compressing with PKLite

The "-o" option lets you skip this prompt. If the new file already exists, the program overwrites it automatically.

```
PKLITE -o MODE.COM CMODE:COM
```

The "-b" option is the opposite of the "-o" option because it provides added security against the possibility of accidental file destruction. Remember, PKLite usually overwrites the original file with the compressed version.

```
PKLITE MODE.COM
```

The above command creates a compressed version of MODE.COM and saves it under the same name. Therefore, the original version is lost. To prevent this from happening, use the "-b" option.

```
PKLITE -b MODE.COM
```

With this command, the compressed file is saved as MODE.COM, like before. However, now the original is saved as a backup version called "MODE.BAK." If you still want to run this version, you must rename it. However, don't call it MODE.COM because this name already exits.

```
REN MODE.BAK OLDMODE.COM
```

You can control whether PKLite updates the compressed program's time stamp. It will be updated to the current date and time if the "-u" option is specified. Otherwise, it remains as is. You might want to use this option to differentiate multiple copies of the same compressed program.

```
PKLITE -u MODE.COM
```

The above command compresses the MODE program and updates its time stamp. Extract protection involves an intensive compression process that results in a smaller than usual file. More importantly, the "-x" (extract) option cannot subsequently be used to decompress the program. The "-e" option provides extract protection. However, this option isn't supported by the shareware version of PKLite.

EXE files usually contain certain information that isn't needed by the program. This data takes up valuable memory space. With PKLite, you can use the "-r" option to remove this information.

```
PKLITE -r NEWPROG.EXE
```

Use this option carefully, since the data will be permanently deleted. It cannot be reconstructed, even by using the "-x" option to decompress the file.

Also, other programs sometimes use this information. For example, a debugger needs it to interpret internal data structures and addresses.

Overlays

As we mentioned, overlays and program compression don't always mix. When you try to compress a program that has overlays, PKLite usually reports this and asks whether it should continue.

You can prevent this from happening by using the "-a" option, which tells PKLite to always proceed with compression, even if overlays are present.

> When you use this option, save the compressed version under a separate name. For example:
>
> ```
> PKLITE -a BIGPROG.EXE SMALL.EXE
> ```

With the "-n" option, you can tell PKLite never to proceed with compression if overlays are present:

```
PKLITE -n BIGPROG.EXE
```

Decompressing programs

Programs that were compressed by PKLite can also be decompressed to their original form. The "-x" option decompresses the data and removes the decompression module from the file:

```
PKLITE -x MODE.COM
```

If the specified file wasn't compressed, PKLite realizes this and displays a warning message.

Many software developers use compression as a way to protect their programs. Since it is a type of encryption, it protects copyright information, copy-protection schemes, and other important data from tampering. However, such protection is canceled if anyone can simply restore the original code by using the "-x" option. The "-e" option prevents this by providing extract protection. As we mentioned, this option isn't available in the shareware version. It's well worth the cost of registration to obtain the full version.

Options

The following table provides an overview of all the options available in PKLite. The syntax is as follows:

```
PKLITE [Options] [Path]PROG [[Path]NEWPROG]
```

Option	Meaning
-a	Always compress, even if program has overlays.
-b	Save a backup of the original file renamed as .BAK.
-e	Compress in such a way that decompression isn't permitted.
-l	Display license screen.
-n	Do not compress a program that has overlays.
-o	Overwrite the target file if it already exists, without prompting for confirmation.
-r	Remove extraneous data from an EXE file. The data cannot later be restored, even with the "-x" parameter.
-u	Update time stamp to current date and time.
-x	Extract (decompress) program to original form.

DIET

The DIET program, written by Teddy Matsumoto of Japan, is the most comprehensive EXE compressor. This program can process data files as well as programs.

If you think of DIET as a cross between PKLite and PKZIP, you're partially right. However, this program offers much more. Data files compressed by traditional compression programs must be restored to their original form before they can be used. However, this isn't necessary in DIET. If you install DIET as a sort of monitor in memory, it starts the data transfer process and decompresses compressed files as they are read from the disk, right into memory.

Now you can leave even your large data files permanently compressed. Whenever a program accesses one of these files, DIET automatically performs the required manipulations.

To be able to do this, DIET must constantly monitor the flow of data to and from the disk. This means it must remain memory-resident in order to compress and decompress data automatically.

Besides this permanent monitoring function, DIET can be used in nonresident mode to handle the various batch operations of a conventional file archiver. This includes compressing programs into executable archives.

In the following sections, we'll explain how to use DIET, both as a freestanding file compressor and as a memory-resident module.

Compressing files

DIET works with all types of files. COM, EXE, and ordinary data files are all supported. Let's start by reviewing DIET's functions. To do this, call the program without any parameters:

```
DIET
```

One of the easiest archiving tasks is compressing the entire current directory. To do this, enter the following:

```
DIET *.*
```

You can also specify which files you want to compress:

```
DIET *.EXE

DIET PROF.TXT

DIET TEXTS.TXT EXTRA.XLS
```

The first command compresses all EXE program files in the current directory. The second compresses a single file called PROF.TXT, and the last one compresses two named files together.

171

```
C:\>diet
<<<< exciting file slimming exerciser 'DIET' version 1.44 >>>>
      .... copyright(c) 1992,1/22  by Teddy Matsumoto ....

Usage:  DIET [option] filename [filename]...

-X        compress as executable file        -L      list out DIET files
-D        compress as data file              -H      check DIET files
-R        retrieve data files                -L      check original DIET.EXE
-RA       retrieve all files                 -B      compare by byte size
-G        choose great SFX routine           -I      ignore warnings
-K        kill tmporary file at program end  -J      JAPANESE message
-$        compress recorded files manually   -A      set R/O attribute

-Z[n] stay on memory  (n=0,1,2:EMS mode)     -P      recompress melted files
      / change status (if already stayed)    -W      compress newly created files
-ZR       remove from memory                 -N      not compress automatically
-ZA       activate TSR function   (DIET ON ) -M      no message output
-ZD       deactivate TSR function (DIET OFF) -S      set original file size

-Cxxxx     copy files with compressing/retrieving (check timestamp)
-Oxxxx     output file / directory designation
-Txxxx     temporary file directory designation

C:\>
```

DIET help screen

DIET doesn't preserve the original files. However, you can add the "-O" option to compress them under new names or in a different location:

```
DIET -O*.BAK *.TXT
```

The above command compresses all .TXT files found in the current directory. Instead of storing these files under the original names, it creates new copies, which have the .BAK extension. This method isn't very useful for COM and EXE files because they need their extensions in order to run. In this case, you can place the new files in a different directory:

```
DIET -OC:\NEWVER\ *.EXE *.COM
```

All programs in the current directory are compressed and placed in the directory called "C:\NEWVER." Remember that the path must end with a backslash. If this is missing, DIET displays the following message:

```
C:\>diet -oc:\newver *.exe *.com
<<<< exciting file slimming exerciser 'DIET' version 1.44 >>>>
       .... copyright(c) 1992,1/22  by Teddy Matsumoto ....

Compress 'COMMAND.COM' to 'C:\NEWVER' .......................
- Disk I/O error!


C:\>
```

The target directory must also exist because it won't be created automatically. The next illustration shows a feature of DIET that isn't included with other compression programs:

```
C:\>diet *.com
<<<< exciting file slimming exerciser 'DIET' version 1.44 >>>>
       .... copyright(c) 1992,1/22  by Teddy Matsumoto ....

Compress 'FORMAT.COM' ..........
Success! (40135 to 19145 bytes)

Compress 'EDIT.COM' .................
Success! (69886 to 47476 bytes)

Compress 'COMMAND.COM' .......................
Success! (92870 to 44365 bytes)


C:\>
```

Programs are compressed

DIET *.COM

As you see from the command, all COM programs in the current directory are compressed and saved under the original names. The illustration above shows that most of the files were compressed. DIET reports the compression wasn't successful for DOSKEY.COM and MORE.COM.

173

This "failure" indicates how DIET evaluates the outcome of compression. In this case, the memory space needed on the storage medium is considered instead of the size of a file itself. This is due to a basic disk management unit called the cluster. While a diskette cluster is 512 bytes, units of 2048 or even 4096 may be used on hard drives. The data for a file is stored in a series of clusters. It's not possible for a file to take up less than one cluster on a disk. For example, on our hard drive, with a cluster size of 2K, a 12-byte file would require a full 2K.

Now let's return to DIET. The program doesn't consider compression a success unless the compressed version uses fewer clusters than the original. This is the only value that represents a usable gain in disk space. The two files that weren't compressed successfully have the following values (with the 2K cluster size, both files again used the same number of clusters after compression):

File	Before	After	Space saved
EDIT.COM	69,886	47,476	22,410
FORMAT.COM	40,135	19,145	20,990

```
C:\>diet -b edit.com format.com
<<<< exciting file slimming exerciser 'DIET' version 1.44 >>>>
       .... copyright(c) 1992,1/22  by Teddy Matsumoto ....

Compress 'EDIT.COM' ..................
Success! (69886 to 47476 bytes)

Compress 'FORMAT.COM' .........
Success! (40135 to 19145 bytes)


C:\>
```

Now the compression is successful

Compressing with the "-b" option tells DIET to evaluate its success by comparing "before" and "after" sizes in bytes instead of clusters. EDIT.COM and FORMAT.COM are considered successfully compressed with the following command:

```
DIET -b EDIT.COM  FORMAT.COM
```

174

Managing files

Since there isn't a special filename extension identifying files compressed by DIET, these files look at first like normal files. Use the "-L" option to determine which files are compressed:

```
DIET -L
```

```
C:\>diet -l
<<<< exciting file slimming exerciser 'DIET' version 1.44 >>>>
      .... copyright(c) 1992,1/22  by Teddy Matsumoto ....

  COMMAND.COM    AUTOEXEC.DOS   CONFIG.DOS    SCANDISK.LOG   ROOT.ZIP
  CONFIG.SYS     TEST.ZIP       AUTOEXEC.BAT  CLASS.PCX      MODE.EXE
 #FORMAT.COM     KEYS.DEB       MODE.BAK      MODE.OLD       CTL3D32.DLL
  LOGO.SYS       V50K.ARJ       CONFIG.WIN    ALAGCAFJ       GRABBER.BAT

C:\>
```

Locating compressed files

Now you can easily see which files were produced by DIET. A number sign (#) precedes each file; if your PC is equipped with the ANSI.SYS driver, the compressed files are highlighted.

DIET can also check compressed files for errors. This function is similar to the CRC testing performed by other compression programs. The letter used for this option is "-h":

```
DIET -h *.*
```

This command checks all files in the current directory. A file mask is required. If one isn't specified, the help screen appears instead.

DIET can even check itself to make sure it is intact. Although DIET wouldn't let us compress it, suppose that another program were to change it somehow. DIET performs a self-test with the "-!" option, so you can make sure the program is still working:

```
DIET -!
```

Compressing problem files

Overlays can present problems for DIET, just as they do for other program compressors. Normally files with overlays are reported to the user and excluded from processing. You can change this by using the "-I" or "-V" option.

```
DIET -V BIG.EXE
```

The above command compresses the program BIG.EXE. If it has overlays, DIET notes this but compresses it anyway.

```
DIET -I BIG.EXE
```

The "-I" option directly affect overlays, but it ignores warnings and exception processing. If you use this parameter, a program with overlays would simply be compressed.

DIET can also compress a special type of program called a device driver. These programs work in the background of your system to control input and output from peripheral devices.

Device drivers have the .SYS filename extension and contain instructions like regular programs. However, instead of being called separately, device drivers are loaded into memory and started when you boot your computer. While the computer is running, they remain in memory to monitor and control certain events. The drivers installed on startup are specified in the CONFIG.SYS file, which, despite its name, is not a device driver. Each device driver is specified in a command that begins as follows:

```
DEVICE=....
```

A popular device driver is HIMEM.SYS, which lets you access to memory beyond 1 Meg:

```
DEVICE=HIMEM.SYS
```

Device drivers are structured differently than COM and EXE programs. For this reason, you must use a special option when compressing them. This is the letter "-D":

```
DIET -d -b *.SYS
```

176

Don't be confused by the "-b" in this command line. Remember, this option simply indicates that you want DIET to compare exact file sizes in bytes when reporting whether the compression was successful.

Something else is also confusing. HIMEM.SYS is compressed as a device driver, but CONFIG.SYS, although it has the .SYS extension, isn't. To make this more confusing, CONFIG.SYS can be compressed with the normal command

```
DIET CONFIG.SYS
```

while this returns an error for HIMEM.SYS. The reason why this occurs is actually quite simple. DIET examines a file before compressing it. If the "-D" option is used, the file must be a device driver, which is indicated by the value 255 255 (or FF FF) in the first two data bytes. CONFIG.SYS doesn't have these bytes. This is easily seen by displaying its contents:

```
TYPE CONFIG.SYS
```

CONFIG.SYS is just a simple text file.

```
C:\>type config.sys
DEVICE=C:\DOS\SETVER.EXE
FILES=50
BUFFERS=10,0
SHELL=C:\DOS\COMMAND.COM C:\DOS\  /p
DEVICE=C:\DOS\HIMEM.SYS
DEVICE=C:\DOS\EMM386.EXE NOEMS
DEVICE=C:\DOS\ANSI.SYS
DEVICE=C:\DOS\CONFIG.SYS
DOS=HIGH,UMB
DEVICEHIGH=C:\DOS\DBLSPACE.SYS /MOVE

C:\>
```

Displaying CONFIG.SYS

Using a driver after compression is very easy. If the compressed version remains in the original directory, you don't have to do anything at all. The CONFIG.SYS entry references the same filename, which hasn't changed. Special parameters aren't required.

177

If you put the compressed version in a different directory, however, you must change the path in your CONFIG.SYS file. For example, use the drivers ANSI.SYS and COUNTRY.SYS. Your CONFIG.SYS file has the corresponding commands:

```
...
DEVICE=C:\DOS\ANSI.SYS
DEVICE=C:\DOS\COUNTRY.SYS
...
```

So, the original drivers are in the DOS directory on your C: drive. Now suppose that you create compressed versions of both drivers in the root directory and want to use them:

```
DIET -D -OC:\ C:\DOS\ANSI.SYS C:\DOS\COUNTRY.SYS
```

The CONFIG.SYS entries must be changed as follows:

```
...
DEVICE=C:\ANSI.SYS
DEVICE=C:\COUNTRY.SYS
...
```

Remember, the new versions won't be implemented until you reboot your computer. Also, you shouldn't try this without having a boot diskette available, in case something goes wrong.

Compressing device drivers can only save disk space, not memory. The file itself may be smaller, but when you call the driver, the code is decompressed as it loads into memory. If you want to compress your device drivers, make sure you actually reduce the number of clusters and don't retain any original versions. Otherwise you won't save any disk space.

Decompressing files

The compression process can also be reversed. The "-R" option is used for this, combined with the "A" option, if desired.

Option	Meaning
-R	Reverses compression for specified data files (not programs or drivers).
-RA	Reverses compression for all files specified (including programs and drivers).

A file filter must be included in the command:

178

```
DIET -R *.*
```

Although the above command specifies all files, only data files are actually decompressed. COM, EXE, and SYS files ("true" SYS files, not CONFIG.SYS) are skipped. If there are no compressed data files in the current directory, DIET displays the following message:

```
C:\>DIET -R *.*
<<<< exciting file slimming exerciser 'DIET' version 1.44 >>>>
     .... copyright(c) 1992,1/22  by Teddy Matsumoto ....

No files to be processed!

C:\>
```

If the -L command indicates that the directory contains compressed files, try this command again but use the "A" option:

```
DIET -RA *.*
```

This reverses all compressed files, regardless of type, to their original format.

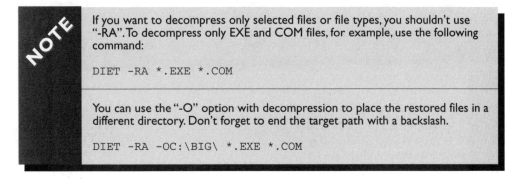

NOTE

If you want to decompress only selected files or file types, you shouldn't use "-RA". To decompress only EXE and COM files, for example, use the following command:

```
DIET -RA *.EXE *.COM
```

You can use the "-O" option with decompression to place the restored files in a different directory. Don't forget to end the target path with a backslash.

```
DIET -RA -OC:\BIG\ *.EXE *.COM
```

179

Memory resident DIET

We mentioned at the beginning of this chapter DIET's memory-resident capabilities for handling compressed files. Now we'll take a closer look at how this works. DIET can function as an extension of MS-DOS, so that it interacts in any exchange of data between memory and the disk. In order to do this, it must be installed as resident in RAM. All options for using DIET in resident mode begin with "Z." To install the program permanently in memory, use the following command:

```
DIET -Z
```

DIET will load into memory and stay there permanently. A program capable of doing this is referred to as a "terminate and stay resident" program, which is abbreviated as TSR. From now on, it monitors all read operations. A message like the following indicates that the installation was successful:

```
C:\>DIET -Z
<<<< exciting file slimming exerciser 'DIET' version 1.44 >>>>
    .... copyright(c) 1992,1/22  by Teddy Matsumoto ....

Stayed on memory!
    melted file          : original
    created file         : original
    compress operation   : automatic
    message output       : on
    file size setting    : compressed file size
    temporary directory  : C:\WINDOWS\TEMP\

C:\>
```

Any message other than "Stayed in Memory!" indicates that a problem has occurred. The items "auto recompress" and "temporary directory" can be changed with parameters. We'll discuss this in more detail later.

When you install any code as memory-resident, you should determine how much space it takes away from other programs. To do this, use the DOS command MEM:

```
MEM /C | MORE
```

The /C parameter displays a table of all the programs currently in memory. DIET will be one of the entries:

```
Modules using memory below 1 MB:

Name         Total              Conventional        Upper Memory
--------    --------------      --------------      --------------
SYSTEM       19,920   (19K)      10,560   (10K)       9,360    (9K)
HIMEM         1,168    (1K)       1,168    (1K)           0    (0K)
EMM386        4,320    (4K)       4,320    (4K)           0    (0K)
ANSI          4,320    (4K)       4,320    (4K)           0    (0K)
WIN           3,696    (4K)       3,696    (4K)           0    (0K)
vmm32        88,000   (86K)         560    (1K)      87,440   (85K)
COMMAND       7,520    (7K)       7,520    (7K)           0    (0K)
GRABBER      16,144   (16K)      16,144   (16K)           0    (0K)
DIET         25,904   (25K)      25,904   (25K)           0    (0K)
D011V200     20,384   (20K)           0    (0K)      20,384   (20K)
IFSHLP        2,864    (3K)           0    (0K)       2,864    (3K)
SETVER          832    (1K)           0    (0K)         832    (1K)
DOSKEY        4,688    (5K)           0    (0K)       4,688    (5K)
Free        580,832  (567K)     580,832  (567K)           0    (0K)

Memory Summary:

Type of Memory      Total         Used          Free
--------------    ----------    ----------    ----------
Press any key to continue . . .
```

Your listing may look a little different, but DIET should occupy 25K.

Temporary directory

Like other compressors, DIET needs extra temporary storage space to do its work. This normally goes in the current directory. With diskette operations you may want to change this, since diskette access is slow and space is limited.

You can specify a temporary directory by using the "-T" option with the installation command:

```
DIET -Z -TC:\WINDOWS\TEMP\
```

The above command tells DIET to use the directory C:\WINDOWS\TEMP\ for any work that requires data swapping.

The ending backslash is required. Now the installation response from DIET will show the specified work directory:

```
temp. directory: C:\WINDOWS\TEMP\
```

You must ensure that the directory exists. Although DIET shows the path you specified, it doesn't actually check for it. It simply assumes that it exists.

Deactivating DIET

There are two ways to deactivate DIET after installing it as memory-resident:

❖ Remove it from memory.

❖ Deactivate it temporarily, but keep it in memory so that it can be reactivated at any time.

Obviously, the most extreme method is to remove DIET from memory. The "R" option is used for this:

```
DIET -ZR
```

The response should be:

```
C:\>DIET -ZR
<<<< exciting file slimming exerciser 'DIET' version 1.44 >>>>
     .... copyright(c) 1992,1/22  by Teddy Matsumoto ....

Removed from memory!

C:\>
```

If you activate this command when the program isn't memory-resident, the response is:

```
C:\>DIET -ZR
<<<< exciting file slimming exerciser 'DIET' version 1.44 >>>>
       .... copyright(c) 1992,1/22  by Teddy Matsumoto ....

Not stayed on memory!

C:\>
```

It's also possible to switch off DIET's monitoring function temporarily and then reactivate it later. The "D" option is used for this:

```
DIET -ZD
```

DIET responds with the following message:

```
C:\>DIET -ZD
<<<< exciting file slimming exerciser 'DIET' version 1.44 >>>>
       .... copyright(c) 1992,1/22  by Teddy Matsumoto ....

TSR function is deactivated!

C:\>
```

Once placed on standby, the program can be called back to work at any time by using the "A" option:

```
DIET -ZA
```

183

DIET indicates that it's ready to work by displaying an appropriate message. The auto recompress and temp directory settings are also shown.

After you install DIET with the "-Z" option, the background monitoring mode usually is activated immediately. If it's not working, try activating it manually:

```
DIET -ZA
```

Sometimes DIET deactivates itself. This can happen when the user interrupts a compression or decompression process by pressing Ctrl+Break or Ctrl+C. You can reactivate it using "-ZA".

As we explained, DIET automatically intervenes in the DOS process of reading a file. When a program writes to the file, however, the data isn't necessarily compressed as it goes to the disk. If you want this to happen, you must specify the "-P" option.

```
DIET -Z -P
```

The above command activates the auto recompress mode. You can use this command to install the program or after it's already resident. In the latter case, DIET is not actually reloaded.

Unfortunately, the Recompress function isn't completely reliable. Some programs won't work with it properly, so they still write data in uncompressed form. You should check your files after one of these programs has used them. If they aren't compressed, simply compress them with the usual command:

```
DIET *.DOC
```

When a problem occurs with write compression, DIET reports an error. You can suppress error messages with the "-M" option:

```
DIET -Z -P -M
```

Example

We'll use an example to demonstrate this process. First, we'll compress a file. We've chosen ABACAT.DOC, a simple text file. The figure below shows the contents of the file before it's compressed.

```
MORE<ABACAT.DOC
```

184

```
C:\>more<abacat.doc

To: All Persons:

This is just a note tp remind you to register all the shareware products
that are included with the companion CD-Rom in the book titled

The Zip Bible

Thank you,

Abacus Editorial and Technical Departments

C:\>
```

Contents of a text file

Now we can perform the compression:

```
DIET -b ABACAT.DOC
```

Since the file is already less than one cluster, DIET won't consider it successfully compressed unless we also use the "-b" option. Now the program will compare the before and after sizes in bytes instead of clusters.

```
C:\>more<abacat.doc

L=!¥ædlz ± ⌐θ ∩
To: All Perso┤ns:€∞his    ²just a note  ∩to remind you≥g┃ ⊤r■?Å┬th ┃sha∞■?ω" produ
cts∥⟨┃õa╛ø!♀┃clude┬wi∞⊤▼┬companiî ├ CD-ROM fo┤⊤⟩îbook≈ilñn∝ds'r∞ZiⱭGp Bible''ᴸw┃┃
┃x,≥─╥⍺AbacS E☺ᴸdó┃┃inîW? Techfc⟩∩⏃Staffq
C:\>
```

Garbage characters

The compressed file is now unreadable to an ordinary program. We can see this by trying to read its contents again by using MORE.

As expected, all we see are "garbage" characters.

Now we'll install DIET in memory-resident mode.

```
DIET -Z
DIET -ZA
```

The first command performs the installation, and the second one ensures that the program is activated. Now things have changed. A third attempt to read ABACAT.DOC, without explicitly decompressing it first, works without any problems:

```
MORE<ABACAT.DOC
```

DIET parameters

The following screen shows and defines the parameters you can use with DIET:

```
D:\PACKDISK>diet
<<<< exciting file slimming exerciser 'DIET' version 1.44 >>>>
      .... copyright(c) 1992,1/22  by Teddy Matsumoto ....

Usage:  DIET [option] filename [filename]...

-X      compress as executable file          -L      list out DIET files
-D      compress as data file                -H      check DIET files
-R      retrieve data files                  -L      check original DIET.EXE
-RA     retrieve all files                   -B      compare by byte size
-G      choose great SFX routine             -I      ignore warnings
-K      kill tmporary file at program end    -J      JAPANESE message
-$      compress recorded files manually     -A      set R/O attribute

-Z[n] stay on memory  (n=0,1,2:EMS mode)     -P      recompress melted files
      / change status (if already stayed)    -W      compress newly created files
-ZR   remove from memory                     -N      not compress automatically
-ZA   activate TSR function  (DIET ON )      -M      no message output
-ZD   deactivate TSR function (DIET OFF)     -S      set original file size

-Cxxxx    copy files with compressing/retrieving (check timestamp)
-Oxxxx    output file / directory designation
-Txxxx    temporary file directory designation

D:\PACKDISK>
```

Command Summary And Switches

ERRORLEVEL basics

ERRORLEVEL is a variable that can be tested following program execution to determine whether certain problems occurred. This approach is used in batch mode, where a program cannot interact with the user by sending error messages directly to the screen.

If you use compression programs in batch files, you should check for errors immediately after each command. Be careful about testing

In this chapter, we'll summarize the features of each of the compression programs we discussed in this book. As you'll see, these programs provide a variety of options, especially ARJ.

Each section is divided into syntax, commands and switches (or options). When needed, we used examples to clarify the information.

values with the DOS IF command. This command works differently than the same command in a normal programming language.

You're probably familiar with programming statements like the following:

```
IF Errorlevel = 20 Then ...

IF Errorlevel = 25 Then ...
```

Each of the above examples tests the variable for an exact value. Coding the same task for DOS is less straightforward. DOS performs a greater-or-equal test on the value of Errorlevel. We'll use an example to demonstrate the implications of this test.

Suppose that a program can return any code from 0 through 10. If you're interested in a value of 3, you must eliminate the other possibilities. Here's how it works:

```
ARJ a PAN Peter.*
IF Errorlevel 4 ECHO Unimportant error
IF Errorlevel 3 GOTO Important
IF Errorlevel 1 ECHO Unimportant error
IF Errorlevel 0 ECHO No error
```

The first line checks for codes greater than or equal to 4. The next line checks for codes greater than or equal to 3, but everything greater than 3 has already been eliminated. Consequently, if this condition is true, we know that the code equals 3.

Not all programs return a specific code for each possible outcome. However, the value 0 is almost always used to indicate error-free execution, while other values mean that something went wrong. A batch file that checks for successful completion of an operation might contain the following lines:

```
...
LHA e GAMES *.* C:\GAMES
IF Errorlevel 1 GOTO Error
ECHO Extract successful
```

ARJ 2.41 Commands

Syntax

```
ARJ <Command> [-<Switch>[-/+]<Switch>]...] <Archivename>[.ARJ] [<filenames>...]
```

Please note the following concerning the syntax:

❖ No distinction is made between upper and lowercase characters.

❖ Switches may be placed anywhere after the command letter.

❖ Entries enclosed in square brackets ([]) aren't required.

Restrictions

Although you probably won't encounter them in everyday use, the following restrictions apply to ARJ:

- ❖ 64 filenames or wildcards per command line.

- ❖ 16,000 filenames resulting from the use of wildcards.

- ❖ 8,000 filenames or wildcards to be excluded.

- ❖ 8,000 ARJ filenames resulting from the use of wildcards.

- ❖ 2,048 characters per comment (25 lines or a comment file of up to 2,048 characters).

Memory requirements

ARJ takes up a lot of memory, especially when operating in its most intensive compression mode. This takes about 290,000 bytes, while extracting files from an archive takes about 166,000 bytes.

Memory limitation is the reason for the 16,000 file restriction noted above.

Commands

The following is the complete command reference for ARJ. As you can see by the number of commands that are provided, ARJ is a versatile and powerful program.

We've divided this section into two parts:

1. Commands

    All the command letters of ARJ are listed alphabetically. The explanation of the command may include cross-references to related commands or switches.

2. Switches

    Switches modify commands. Since there are so many switches, it's not practical to list the applicable ones with each individual command. Therefore, they are arranged alphabetically in a separate section.

a	add

Add places the specified files into an archive. Files with the same names are overwritten.

Examples:

```
ARJ a archive
```

Compresses all files from the current drive and directory into the archive file called ARCHIVE.ARJ.

```
ARJ a e:\pics\graphics c:\windows\*.bmp
```

Compresses all files ending in ".BMP", from the WINDOWS directory on the C: drive, into an archive file called GRAPHICS.ARJ in the PICS directory on the E: drive.

```
ARJ a -r -vv1440K b:\archive c:\*.*
```

Compresses all files from drive C: into the archive file(s) ARCHIVE.ARJ (A01, A02, ...) on 3.5-inch, 1.44 Meg diskettes in drive B:.

The **Add** command allows for a multi-volume archive with up to 99 extension volumes. A beep sounds with each prompt for a new formatted diskette in drive B:.

b	batch command

The "b" command lets you temporarily extract archived files for processing with DOS commands or programs. For example, you can use this command to check the contents of an archived file with the DOS TYPE command.

The extracted files receive the default names ARJTEMP.XXX (XXX represents a series of numbers beginning with 001). The temporary files are deleted when the operation is complete.

Examples:

```
ARJ b archive *.TXT
```

Enter system command: type *.TXT

The above command temporarily extracts all .TXT files from the ARCHIVE.ARJ archive and displays their contents on the screen. The TYPE command is entered after the following prompt:

Enter system command:

The following switches can be used with this command:

-jw	Rename extracted files	-jq	Execute command

```
ARJ b archive chess.pas -jwCheckmat.pas "-jqTURBO Checkmat.pas"
```

This command temporarily extracts the file called "CHESS.PAS" from the archive called "ARCHIVE." The temporary file is then renamed from "ARJTEMP.001" to "CHECKMAT.PAS." Finally, a program called "TURBO" is called to process CHECKMAT.PAS.

c	comment

This command lets you attach comments to archives themselves or to individual files within archives. There are two modes for attaching comments:

❖ You can type up to 25 lines directly in dialog mode. Terminate the entry by pressing [Enter] to create a blank line.

❖ You can pass a previously created text, of up to 2,048 bytes, to the specified archive file using the "-z" switch.

Examples:

```
ARJ c archive
```

The above command activates the dialog mode for entering comments, first for the archive itself and then for each packed file.

```
ARJ c archive -z
```

Only a comment for the archive file is requested.

```
ARJ c archive -zNOTES.TXT
```

The contents of NOTES.TXT (maximum 2,048 bytes) is automatically attached as commentary to the archive.

```
ARJ c archive -zNUL
```

Attaches the contents of the NUL file as commentary to the archive. Since NUL is empty, this deletes any current comments.

```
ARJ c archive -jzNUL
```

Deletes all comments for individual archived files.

```
ARJ c archive -zNUL -jzNUL
```

Deletes all comments, both for the archive itself and for all individual archived files.

 Comments aren't compressed. Therefore, the more comments you include, the lower the overall compression rate will be for the archive.

d	delete

The "d" command deletes one or more compressed files from an archive.

When wildcards are used with the "-q" switch, a confirmation prompt appears before the deletion of each file.

Examples:

```
ARJ d archive *.TXT
```

All files ending in ".TXT" are deleted from the archive.

```
ARJ d -q archive *.TXT
```

You're asked to confirm each .TXT deletion individually.

e	extract

This command extracts one or more compressed files from the specified archive to the current or specified directory.

You must confirm a safety prompt before an existing file is overwritten. To suppress the prompt and assume a "yes" response, include the -y switch with this command.

Directory information stored in the archive is ignored. This means that every extracted file is placed in the specified directory.

Examples:

```
ARJ e archive
```

All files in the ARCHIVE.ARJ archive are extracted to the current directory.

```
ARJ e -y archive b:\Letters *.TXT
```

192

All files ending in ".TXT" are extracted to the target directory "Letters" on drive B:. Existing files are overwritten without a prompt.

f	freshen

Freshen replaces archived files with more current versions.

A file, from the source disk, that isn't already in the archive won't be added to it. (To do this, use the Update "u" command).

Example:

```
ARJ f -r document *.TXT *.DOC
```

This command freshens the archive called "DOCUMENT" by updating archived files ending in ".TXT" and ".DOC" with newer versions from the current directory and subdirectories.

g	garble files

Garble provides password protection for archived files. Garbled files cannot be decompressed without the correct password.

"g" is used as a command to add password protection to files in an existing archive. To garble the files as they are placed in the archive, use it as a switch ("-g") in combination with the appropriate command (Update, Add, etc.).

Remember the following:

❖ Password protection in ARJ is case-sensitive.

❖ Each file in an archive can have its own password. Usually the number of different passwords is kept to a minimum.

The "g" command can also be combined with the "-g" switch, which lets you type the password directly on the command line.

Example:

```
ARJ g archive -gjoshua
```

By using this command all files in the ARCHIVE.ARJ archive are garbled with the password "joshua."

i	integrity of ARJ.EXE

This command checks the ARJ.EXE program itself and reports a CRC error if a problem occurs.

Example:

```
ARJ i ARJ.exe
```

This command checks the integrity of ARJ.EXE (to detect changes introduced by viruses or other file compressors, for example).

j	join

Join combines two or more archives to make a single archive. It also turns executable SFX archives back into normal archives.

Examples:

```
ARJ j letters texts.arj doc.arj
```

This command combines the archives TEXTS.ARJ and DOC.ARJ into a single archive called "LETTERS.ARJ."

```
ARJ j -r archive *.arj
```

The above command is a simple way to combine all archives from the current directory and subdirectories into a single archive called "ARCHIVE.ARJ."

```
ARJ j games games.exe
```

The executable SFX archive GAMES.EXE is converted to a normal archive called "GAMES.ARJ."

k	delete backups

Archived files designated as backups are deleted with this command. Backup files are extra copies of compressed files within an archive.

Examples:

```
ARJ k backup *.*
```

All files marked as backups in the BACKUP.ARJ archive are deleted.

194

```
ARJ k -q document *.TXT
```

All .TXT files marked as backups in the DOCUMENT.ARJ archive are deleted after you confirm the safety prompt for each file.

l	list

List shows the contents of an archive on the default output device (normally the screen). The compressed files are listed in the order in which they were stored.

-jp	This switch lists the output a page at a time.

Example:

```
ARJ l -jp passcr *.pas
```

All .PAS (Pascal source code) files in the PASSCR.ARJ archive are listed on the screen a page at a time.

An extended variation of the List command is Verbose list (v).

m	move

Move archives the specified files and then deletes the original versions.

A safety prompt doesn't appear before each deletion. For added security, use the "-jt" switch with this command. It ensures that the compressed versions are good before deleting the originals.

-jt	Tests archived files before deleting original versions.

Example:

```
ARJ m dbase *.dbf -r -jt
```

The above command archives all dBase data files from the current directory and subdirectories into an archive called "DBASE.ARJ." After a successful integrity test on the compressed files, it also deletes the originals.

n	rename

Rename assigns new names to archived files.

The new names are assigned in dialog mode. ARJ asks for a new name for each file that's specified. To keep the same name, press Enter.

Example:

```
ARJ n texts *.TXT
```

When this command is activated, you'll be asked to enter a new name for each .TXT file in the TEXTS archive.

o	order archive

This command rearranges the files in an archive. Files specified on the command line are placed at the beginning of the archive. The desired sequence can also be specified in a text file. You cannot use wildcards (*, ?).

Examples:

```
ARJ o archive offers.TXT orders.TXT invoices.TXT
```

The three files specified in this command are moved to the front of the ARCHIVE.ARJ archive. The order of any other files in the archive doesn't change.

```
ARJ o texts !textsort.lst
```

This command rearranges the TEXTS.ARJ archive. The new file sequence is specified in a text file called "TEXTSORT.LST."

p	print to standard output

This command prints the contents of compressed files to the standard output device. Unlike List, which simply indicates which files are present, this command prints the actual contents of the files.

Example:

```
ARJ p document
```

Displays the contents of all files in the DOCUMENT archive on the screen.

```
ARJ p document >NUL
```

The output is nulled. Since the files must first be extracted, this is another way of testing the integrity of the archive.

196

```
ARJ p document >PRN
```

The output is directed to the printer.

r	remove pathnames

This command removes all pathnames for the archived files, leaving only the filenames. If a file isn't specified, paths are removed from all files in the archive.

The Remove command has the same effect on an existing archive as the switch -e has when an archive is created. Paths removed in this way cannot be restored.

Example:

```
ARJ r archive *.TXT
```

Path information is removed from all .TXT files in the ARCHIVE.ARJ archive.

s	sample

Sample displays the contents of an archived file on the screen. This command is similar to the Print (p) command, but the display automatically pauses for a user response after each full screen. Also, lines are truncated after the 79th character and control characters are replaced by question marks.

Example:

```
ARJ s document contract.DOC
```

This command displays the file CONTRACT.DOC from the DOCUMENT archive one screen at a time.

t	test

Test checks the integrity of compressed files within an archive. If a file isn't specified, every file in the archive is tested. If the test fails, a CRC error is reported.

Example:

```
ARJ t imprtant
```

This command tests all files in the IMPRTANT.ARJ archive for error-free compression and storage.

u	update

Update replaces files in an archive with newer versions and adds those not yet present. The time stamp is used to control updating.

Example:

```
ARJ u passcr
```

Compresses all files, in the current directory, that don't exist yet in the PASSCR.ARJ archive or that exist there as older versions.

v	verbose list

Similar to the "l" command, Verbose list provides a listing of an archive's contents. However, complete paths are displayed and the compressed files are numbered sequentially.

The numbers can be used instead of filenames to reference the files.

-#	Switch used to access files by position number.

Examples:

```
ARJ v texts -jp
```

All files in the TEXTS archive are listed along with their sequential position numbers. The display pauses between pages.

```
ARJ e texts -# 3 12
```

The third and twelfth files are extracted from the TEXTS archive.

w	where is text?

This command searches archived files for a particular text string. Case-sensitivity is optional, along with the ability to show the desired string in context by listing additional lines.

The following switches can be used:

-jp	Pause when screen is full.
-jv	Display ASCII character codes 128 to 255 (IBM graphic characters).
-jq	Input search information on command line.

Normal input for this command is interactive through a question-and-answer dialog box.

Examples:

```
ARJ w texts
```

This command asks you to enter the search string and specify case-sensitivity and the number of lines to print. All files in the TEXTS archive are then searched for the string, which is displayed when found.

The search can also be initiated directly from the command line without entering dialog mode. This is done by using the "-jq" switch with the following syntax:

```
-jq<ignore-case><line-count><delimiter><search-text>
```

The required entries are:

Ignore-case	"-" to observe case, "+" to ignore case.
Line-count	Number of lines to print with the specified string.
Delimiter	A separation character between line-count and search-text. Usually a plus or minus sign.
Search-text	The exact string to be located. If this consists of more than one word (if spaces are included), the entire -jq group is enclosed in quotes.

```
ARJ w texts -jq+5+offer
```

This command tells ARJ to search all files in the TEXTS.ARJ archive for the word "offer." Case is ignored. If the search is successful, five lines of text will be displayed along with the located string.

```
ARJ j w texts "-jq+5-invoice nr. 007"
```

Although it's similar to the previous example, this command uses "-" as the text delimiter and includes spaces in the text string.

x	extract extended

This command extracts archived files using complete path information. If a specified directory does not exist, it's created after you confirm the prompt that appears.

Example:

```
ARJ x invoices c:\firms
```

All files from the INVOICES.ARJ archive are extracted, along with their complete path structures, to the FIRMS directory on the C: drive. Archived files may be specified as belonging to subdirectories, such as REPORTS or QUARTER. If this directory structure doesn't exist on the target storage medium, you're asked to confirm that it should be added. The files are then extracted accordingly.

y	copy with new options

This command copies an existing archive and applies new features. It can be used to make a self-extracting (SFX) archive from a normal archive. The original archive is also retained.

Example:

```
ARJ y archive -je
```

With this command, a second copy of ARCHIVE.ARJ is created as a self-extracting archive called "ARCHIVE.EXE."

Switches

A switch modifies an ARJ command in a certain way. There are two types of switches: Normal and extended. An extended switch consists of two letters, the first one being "j." The following applies to all switches:

❖ Case is ignored.

❖ A switch is meaningless without a command (except for the help switch).

❖ A switch can appear anywhere on the command line after the command itself.

-?	Help screen

The question mark displays the entire ARJ help text a screen at a time.

```
ARJ -?
```

--	No more switches

This switch indicates that additional switches won't be found on the command line. You'll need this switch if you use filenames beginning with "-."

Example:

```
ARJ a texts -- -info.TXT
```

The file called "-INFO.TXT" will now be recognized as such and processed by ARJ. Without the "--" switch, ARJ would interpret the filename as a wrongly-coded switch.

-+	environment

This switch disables the standard environment variable ARJ_SW and/or replaces it with another variable.

Example:

```
ARJ a archive -+ARJ_ENV
```

The environment variable ARJ_SW is replaced by ARJ_ENV.

-&	critical error handler

This switch traps critical error messages from the operating system (Abort, Fail, Retry) and invokes custom error handling.

You should use this switch when ARJ is working in "unsupervised" mode.

Example:

```
ARJ a b:\archive -&
```

In case of trouble (e.g., an unreadable sector), a custom routine handles the error, so the archiving process doesn't have to be aborted.

201

-!	alternative list symbol

This switch specifies an alternative character for list file processing (the standard symbol is "!").

Example:

```
ARJ a archive -!@ @sort.lst
```

The standard symbol used by LHA and PKZIP ("@") is defined as the list symbol.

-$	volume name

Adds the name of the current volume (volume label) on the indicated drive to an archive. A single archive can have more than one volume label.

The volume label is displayed with the DOS VOL command.

Example:

```
ARJ u texts -$C:
```

The volume name of the C: drive is added as a file to the TEXTS.ARJ archive.

-#	file number

Selects files in an archive by position number. The verbose list (v) command shows the position number for each file.

Example:

```
ARJ e texts -# 1 5 10 12
```

The first, fifth, tenth, and twelfth files are extracted from the TEXTS.ARJ archive.

-a	file attributes

The file attributesswitch provides access to all files regardless of attributes. With the default setting in ARJ, Hidden and System, files are ignored.

-a	Allow all file attributes.	-a1	Include empty directories.

-b	Backup

When the backup switch is specified, the archiving process checks the backup (archive) attribute of each file to determine the desired processing.

DOS sets this attribute when a file is added or changed. A backup program can then determine which files should be saved and which have remained untouched since the last backup.

-b	Saves only those files whose archive bit is set.
-b1	Saves only those files whose archive bit is set. Clears the bit after archiving is complete.
-b2	Resets the archive bits for the specified files. Unlike -b and -b1, this switch does not in itself serve as a file selector.

Examples:

```
ARJ a a:backup c:\*.TXT -r -b1
```

In the above example, all .TXT files on drive C: that carry the archive attribute are compressed to the BACKUP.ARJ archive on drive A:. The archive bits are cleared as the files are saved. For this reason, files wouldn't be saved on a subsequent execution if the same command was immediately repeated.

```
ARJ a c:backup *.dbf *.xls -b
```

All files in the current directory that carry the archive attribute and end in ".DBF" or ".XLS" are packed to the BACKUP.ARJ archive.

```
ARJ a c:Backup \*.DOC -b2
```

Every .DOC file on the current drive is saved to the BACKUP.ARJ archive regardless of the setting of its archive bit. If the bit was set, it's cleared after the file is saved.

-c	skip time check

This switch eliminates checking of file time stamps. Normally the time stamp controls which files the "f" and "u" commands will save. With the "-c" switch, all files are saved regardless of when they were last updated.

-d	delete

This switch indicates subsequent deletion of selected files. All files processed will be deleted after the associated command is executed.

Example:

```
ARJ a texts *.DOC -d -y
```

All .DOC files will be compressed to the TEXTS.ARJ archive. The originals will be deleted without a safety prompt.

-e	no pathname

This switch eliminates path information from archived files. Only the filename is stored. The "x" command cannot restore the original directory structure.

-e	Do not save paths.	-e1	Do not save output directory.

Example:

```
ARJ a archive c:\dos\*.* -e1
```

All files in the DOS subdirectory are archived without path information (therefore, also without the DOS output directory).

-f	freshen

When used with the "e" or "x" command, this switch ensures that only newer versions of files already present on the target storage medium will be decompressed. When used with the "m" command, this switch ensures that only newer versions of files already present in the archive will be moved to it.

Example:

```
ARJ e texts *.TXT -f
```

A .TXT file will be extracted to the disk, only if it already exists there, but with an older date and time.

-g	garble with password

When used with an archiving command, this switch applies a password to the archived files.

-gXX	Password is entered directly after the switch.	-g?	Password is entered in dialog mode.

This switch is also used to unlock password-protected files from an archive. If the wrong password is used, ARJ reports a CRC error or bad file data.

ARJ is case-sensitive with regard to passwords.

Examples:

```
ARJ a secret c:\private\*.* -gjoshua
```

All files from the PRIVATE subdirectory are packed to the SECRET.ARJ archive and locked with the password "joshua."

```
ARJ a secret c:\private\imprtant.TXT -g?
```

A password is requested in dialog mode (to be entered twice) and applied to the IMPRTANT.TXT file saved in the SECRET.ARJ archive.

```
ARJ e secret -gjoshua
```

All files with the password "joshua" are extracted.

-i	no indicator

With this switch, a progress indicator bar isn't displayed (default setting). By including the "-i1" switch with an archiving command, you can display a bar indicating the progress of the compression process.

-i	Progress indicator not displayed.	-i1	Progress indicator is displayed.

-j	shifted switch

This switch changes the meaning of the switch that follows to its alternative value. For example, "-a" is different from "-ja" but the same as "-jja." The combination "-jae" means the same as "-ja je." Extended switches are listed at the end of this section.

205

-k	backup of archive

This switch creates a backup (.BAK) copy of an archive when it's changed. An existing .BAK file with the same name will be overwritten.

-l	list file

Creates a list file, which is a text file containing the names or wildcards for the files affected by the command.

Examples:

```
ARJ a texts c:\winword\*.DOC *.TXT -llist.TXT
```

After packing all .DOC and .TXT files from the WINWORD directory to the TEXTS.ARJ archive, the program creates a text file containing the filenames selected.

```
ARJ l texts -llist.lst
```

Since this command doesn't specify selected files to be listed, the LIST.LST text file will contain the wildcard string "*.*".

-m	method

Specifies the compression method:

-m0	No compression.	-m3	Still less compression, more improved speed.
-m1	Highest compression (standard).	-m4	Lowest compression, highest speed.
-m2	Somewhat less compression, slightly improved speed.		

Example:

```
ARJ a archive *.* -m4
```

All files are compressed using the fastest processing method and the lowest-density compression.

206

-n	new files

This switch selects only new files. When used with a decompression command, only files not already in the target directory are decompressed. When used with an archiving command, only files not already present in the archive are added to it.

-o	on or after

The "o" switch selects files according to time stamps. You can use it to screen for files of a certain age.

-o	On or after the date-time specified in YYMMDDHHMMSS format.
-ob	Before the date-time specified in YYMMDDHHMMSS format.

By combining both switches, you can define an interval during which a file must have been created or modified. A year less than 80 will be considered in the twenty-first century.

Examples:

```
ARJ a archive -o960101
```

Archives all files created or modified on January 1, 1996 or later.

```
ARJ a archive -o960101 -ob960107
```

Archives all files created or modified from January 1, 1996 to January 7, 1996.

-p	match pathname

If files with the same name exist under different pathnames, you can use this switch to specify the path of the desired file.

-q	query on file

This switch tells ARJ to display a prompt for each file processed. It's especially useful as a safety feature with commands that involve file deleting. You must confirm a query before each file is deleted.

Example:

```
ARJ d document *.DOC -q
```

All .DOC files should be deleted from the DOCUMENT archive. ARJ will ask you to verify each deletion.

-r	recurse subdirs

This switch tells ARJ to recurse all subdirectories encountered during processing of the specified files. This allows you to preserve the original directory structure in the archive.

Appropriate switches:

-a	Hidden and system files will also be archived.
-a1	Empty directories will also be archived.

Examples:

```
ARJ a secure c:\*.bak -r
```

All backup (.BAK) files in the C: root and its underlying subdirectories will be compressed to the SECURE.ARJ archive.

```
ARJ a secure c:\*.bak -r -a -a1
```

Same as above, but hidden and system files as well as empty directories will also be archived.

-s	archive time-stamp

This switch applies the time stamp from the most recently archived file to the archive itself.

-t	file type

The "-t" or "-t0" switch indicates that the specified files should be handled as binary files (the standard setting). With the "-t1" switch, the files are handled as text files.

-u	update

This switch updates and adds new files. When it's used with a decompression command, ARJ extracts only those files not already present in the target directory or whose date-time precedes the archived version.

When the switch is used with the "m" command, only those files not already present in the archive are moved to it.

-v	multiple volume

This switch allows an archive to extend across multiple volumes.

The volumes are identified by sequential numbers assigned when the archive is created. The following variants are possible:

-vv	A beep signals the end-of-volume condition, file size message and prompt for new diskette.
-vw	Files cannot be split between volumes.
-va	ARJ automatically determines the maximum available file space on the specified drive.
-vs	A DOS command is executed before a new diskette is started.
-v360	Creates archives at 360K.
-v720	Creates archives at 720K.
-v1220	Creates archives at 1.2 Meg
-v1440	Creates archives at 1.44 Meg
-vNN	Creates archives at NN bytes

Examples:

```
ARJ a b:\backup c:\*.* -vv1440 -r
```

All files on the C: drive are archived to multiple 3.5-inch HD (1.44 Meg) diskettes on drive B:. A beep sounds when a new diskette is needed. The first volume of the archive is given the suffix ".ARJ", the second ".A01", the third ".A02", etc.

```
ARJ m -v360 -y -jt -r d:\backup c:\*.*
```

The above command initiates the archiving of all files on the C: drive to multiple volumes of 360K on drive D:. The original files are deleted without a prompt, since automatic confirmation is indicated by the "-y" switch.

```
ARJ a b:\backup -vvwasCOMMAND c:\*.TXT -r
```

This command saves all .TXT files from the C: drive to the BACKUP archive on drive B:. Multiple volumes are allowed. Each new volume is signaled by a beep (v), files will not be split (w), disk space is analyzed automatically (a), and COMMAND.COM is executed before each volume (s).

-w	work directory

This switch specifies a work directory that ARJ can use during compression or extraction.

The program can store and manipulate an archive there temporarily, then copy it to the target drive and release the file space when the operation is complete. This usually speeds up processing.

 This technique is especially effective if you place the working directory on a RAMDISK.

Example:

```
ARJ a -we:\ a:\archive *.TXT
```

The .TXT files in this example are compressed temporarily to the E: drive in RAM and subsequently copied to a diskette on drive A:. If copying is interrupted, both the temporary and the target archive are deleted.

-x	exclude files

This switch excludes certain files from processing.

When used with an archiving command, files specified by name or with wildcards after the switch won't be compressed. Multiple names or wildcards are allowed, as is the use of a list file with the "-!" switch.

Examples:

```
ARJ a source *.* -x*.pas -x*.bas
```

All files except Pascal and Basic source files are compressed to the SOURCE.ARJ archive.

```
ARJ a source *.* -x!excl.lst
```

210

The contents of EXCL.LST specifies the files to be excluded.

```
ARJ a passrc c:\tp6\*.pas -r -x\tp6\*.pas
```

It's also possible to completely exclude directories. In fact, you can exclude a directory, and still have its subdirectories compressed. This is what happens in the example shown above. All Pascal files in subdirectories of the C:\TP6 directory are compressed into an archive named "PASSRC.ARJ."

-y	assume yes

All prompts during processing of the associated command are answered "yes" when this switch is used. You should use this switch when ARJ is executing a task automatically.

Example:

```
AUTOARC.EXE -y
```

The self-extracting archive AUTOARC begins extracting files without further prompts.

-z	zipfile comment

Assigns a comment to an archive. When used with the "c" command, this switch assigns commentary to an archive itself, instead of to an individual archived file.

Example:

```
ARJ c hello -zPETER.TXT
```

Assigns the contents of PETER.TXT as a comment to the HELLO archive.

Extended switches

Extended switches are used exactly like normal switches. They are used only because some letters must be duplicated in order to accommodate all the necessary options. An extended switch always begins with "j".

-jb	backup

The -jb group relates to backups of files within archives.

The following variants are possible:

211

-jb	Indicates an archive as a backup archive.
-jb1	Erases the backup indicator for an archive.
-jb2	Erases the backup indicator for an archived file.
-jb3	Indicates an archived file as a backup file.

-jc	exit after count

This switch terminates a command after a certain number of files have been processed.

Examples:

```
ARJ l texts -jc5
```

The first five files from the TEXTS.ARJ archive are listed on the screen.

```
ARJ a texts -jc5
```

The first five files under the current directory are archived to TEXTS.ARJ.

-jd	disk space

This switch ensures that a specified amount of disk space remains free on the target drive when files are extracted. If the limit is reached, ARJ will stop processing and report errors for the files that haven't been extracted yet.

```
ARJ e -jd 100000 archive
```

ARJ extracts as many files as possible from ARCHIVE.ARJ until the available disk space on the target drive falls below 100K.

-je	SFX-archive

This switch creates a self-extracting (SFX) archive. Unlike LHA and PKZIP, ARJ creates the SFX archive during the archiving process. In conjunction with the "y" command, this switch can be used to make a self-extracting archive (.EXE) from a normal archive (.ARJ). The following variants exist:

-je	Creates the normal SFX module
-je1	Creates a SFXJR (SFX Junior) module with limited capabilities and lower memory requirement.

212

-jf	full path

This switch saves the full path of each file that is archived.

-jf	Saves full path.
-jf1	Saves path without drive.

-jg	select backup files

This switch selects archived files marked as backups. This makes it possible to use backup files in operations when they aren't usually accessible. The "k" and "y" commands are the only ones that normally work with backups. With the "-jg" switch, other commands like "e" or "d" can process them as well.

Example:

```
ARJ d -jg backup *.bak
```

All backup files with the suffix .BAK are deleted from the BACKUP.ARJ archive.

-jh	huffman buffer

This switch lets you specify a size for the Huffman buffer.

Buffer size can affect processing speed. So many factors play a role here that experimenting is the best way to determine a reasonable size.

Examples:

```
ARJ a DOC *.TXT -jh2048
```

Here the minimum buffer size of 2,048 bytes is used.

```
ARJ a DOC *.TXT -jh65535
```

Here the buffer is increased to the maximum size of 64K.

-ji	index file

Creates an index file with the specified name.

An index file lists all the files that were selected by a given command. This is especially useful when backing up a lot of data on several diskettes. The index helps you locate a desired file more easily.

Example:

```
ARJ a -jiindex.lst -r pics *.pcx
```

All PCX files archived in PICS.ARJ are listed in an index file called "INDEX.LST". You can display the index later using the TYPE command to locate specific files.

-jk	keep temp archive

This switch retains the temporary archive after an abort or error that would normally delete it. The name of the temporary archive is "ARJTEMP.$00."

-jl	display only filespec

Only file-specific information is displayed with this switch. Path and drive designations are suppressed to make the screen easier to read.

-jm	maximum compression

ARJ assumes an enhanced compression (tighter packing) mode with this switch.

-jm works in conjunction with "-m1" or "-m2." Compression is noticeably slower, however. About 1% to 8% higher compression is usually possible.

Use of the -jm switch with -m3 and -m4 is undefined.

-jn	restart at

This switch is used to specify a file at which a previously interrupted multi-volume archiving can be resumed. It's used in conjunction with "-jx."

Example:

```
ARJ a archive -v360 -r -jn\pascal\turbo.exe -jx1000
```

214

The above command skips all files up to TURBO.EXE and resumes archiving from there, starting with file position 1000.

-jo	query/unique

ARJ interprets this switch differently for compressing versus unpacking procedures.

In connection with the "m" or "a" command, it queries the user before overwriting archived files.

With extracting commands, it generates a unique extension where needed to avoid duplicate filenames in the target directory.

Numeric extensions from 000 to 999 are used.

-jp	pause after screen

A command that fills the screen will pause before continuing when this switch is used.

Example:

```
ARJ v whole -jp
```

-jr	set string parameter

This switch is used to input search information on the command line.

-jr	recover archive

This switch is used for recovering data from defective archives.

In a CRC failure or "Bad file data" error, part of the archive may be salvaged using "-jr."

Example:

```
ARJ e -jr archiv
```

The above command tries to extract data from the archive in spite of errors.

-js	store by suffix

This switch specifies, by suffix, certain types of files that should be archived without compression.

Normally this switch is used to avoid trying to compress files that are already in compressed form.

 NOTE
ARJ, ZIP, LZH, PAK, and ARC are the default suffixes for this option. Other types of files can be stored without compression by specifying the appropriate endings.

Example:

```
ARJ a uncomp -js.arj.lzh.gif.tif
```

All files with the specified suffixes are stored in the UNCOMP.ARJ archive in their current form.

-jt	test temp archive

ARJ tests a new archive before deleting existing files when this switch is specified. If an error occurs, the original data won't be overwritten or deleted. You can also use this switch to do an integrity check on an archive before extracting files from it. If an error occurs, the files won't be extracted.

Example:

```
ARJ m archive -jt
```

Before deleting the originals, ARJ checks the compressed files for errors.

```
ARJ e archive -jt
```

Before extracting the compressed files, ARJ checks them for errors.

-jv	verbose display

This switch calls for detailed screen output when used with the "t" or "x" command. When used with the "v" command, compressed files are shown without paths.

-jw	extract output name

You can use this switch in an extract command to specify an output device.

216

Example:

```
ARJ e texts appl.TXT -jwPRN
```

The APPL.TXT file is sent to the printer.

-jx	extended position

This switch lets you resume processing at a particular file position.

A multi-volume archiving procedure that aborted with an error can be continued from the file where the interruption occurred. You restart the process by manually entering the correct file position with this switch. An interrupted restore (extraction) can be similarly resumed.

Example:

```
ARJ a archive1.a01 readme.TXT -jx100000
```

The above command contains a manual restart command for the archiving of the README.TXT file at position 100000 on the ARCHIVE1.A01 volume.

-jy	assume yes

This switch indicates an automatic "yes" response for certain questions. The "-jy" switch is much more limited than the "-y" switch. The specific question that is to be confirmed is coded along with the switch.

The following can be specified:

a	APPEND when extracting split files.	o	Overwrite existing file.
c	Create directory.	r	Delete keyboard buffer.
d	Delete file.	s	Text search.
k	Available memory.	v	Multi-volume archiving.
n	New filename.	y	Accept letter responses (Y/N/A/Q).

Example:

```
ARJ x archive -v -jyaco
```

This command suppresses the questions for appending files, creating directories, and overwriting files and assumes that all these actions are permitted.

217

-jz	zipfile comment

This switch indicates that a comment refers to an individual file in an archive. It's closely related to the "-z" (archive comment) switch and the "c" command.

Examples:

```
ARJ c archive TOC.TXT -jzcomment.TXT
```

The above command assigns a comment, which is taken from a file called COMMENT.TXT, to the TOC.TXT file in ARCHIVE.ARJ.

```
ARJ c archive *.TXT -jzNUL
```

The comments for all .TXT files in ARCHIVE.ARJ are deleted.

ERRORLEVELS

The following table shows which error codes ARJ may return in the ERRORLEVEL variable. A batch file can check the value of this variable.

Code	Meaning
0	No error
1x	Warning Specified file not found, NO to continue query
2	Fatal error
3	CRC failure Archive or archived file
4	ARJ integrity error Registered version only
5	Disk full or write error
6	Cannot open archive or file
7	User error, wrong parameter
8	Insufficient memory

LHA 2.13 Commands

Syntax

```
LHA <Command> [/<option> ARC [[DIR\] [File]...]... [-+012ºWDIR]...]
```

Commands

a	add

Adds files to the specified archive. Existing files are overwritten regardless of age. If the archive doesn't exist, it's created.

LHA assigns the suffix ".LZH" to an archive, unless directed otherwise. If the archive already exists, it's overwritten.

Examples:

```
LHA a program *.exe
```

The above command compresses all .EXE files in the current drive and directory to the archive called "PROGRAM.LZH."

```
LHA a -x texts c:\word5\*.TXT
```

This command also saves the complete path data.

d	delete

Deletes one or more files from an archive. Wildcards are permitted.

Example:

```
LHA d document info.DOC control.DOC
```

The two files INFO.DOC and CONTROL.DOC are deleted from the DOCUMENT.LZH archive.

e	extract

Specified files are extracted from an archive to the specified target directory. If the file already exists in the target directory, and if it has the same time stamp or a more recent one than on the archive, the file isn't extracted.

This command is the same as "x", except that path information isn't extracted. To restore the directory structure, use "x."

Example:

```
LHA e archive c:\exefile\*.exe
```

All .EXE files from the ARCHIVE.LZH archive are decompressed to the EXEFILE directory on drive C:.

f	freshen

Updates archived files.

If the date-time of the specified file is more recent than the archived version, the archived version is updated. The "-c" option ignores the time stamp and updates every file.

Example:

```
LHA f texts *.TXT
```

All .TXT files carrying a more recent date-time than the compressed versions in the archive are updated.

l	list

Lists archive contents in table format on the standard output device.

You can bypass the standard output device to create a list file.

Example:

```
LHA l games > List.dat
```

The above command lists the contents of the GAMES archive. Instead of being sent to the screen, the output is sent to a file called "LIST.DAT."

220

m	move

Moves files to an archive (after compressing them) and deletes the original versions if the operation is successful.

Example:

```
LHA m document *.DOC *.TXT
```

Files ending in ".DOC" and ".TXT" are compressed and placed in an archive called "DOCUMENT.LZH." Then the originals are deleted.

p	print to standard output

Prints the contents of one or more archived files on the standard output device.

Examples:

```
LHA p doc info.TXT
```

This command prints the compressed file INFO.TXT to the screen. Unexpected results may occur (beeps, missing characters, etc.) if certain control characters are included.

```
LHA p doc info.TXT >prn
```

Sends the file contents to a connected printer.

s	make SFX-archive

Converts an existing archive to a self-extracting archive. May be used with the following switches:

-x0	Default: Creates a small SFX module with restricted capabilities.
-x1	Creates a larger SFX module that includes path information.

Example:

```
LHA s texts
```

With this command, an executable archive called "TEXTS.EXE" is created from the normal archive TEXTS.LZH.

t	test archive

Tests the integrity of normal and executable archives.

The program LHA.EXE itself can also be tested. To do this, change to the directory that contains LHA.EXE, and type the command "LHA t LHA.EXE." If no errors or changes are found, the following message appears:

This file seems to be ORIGINAL distributed from H. Yoshi.

Examples:

```
LHA t archive
```

The ARCHIVE.LZH archive is tested for errors.

```
LHA t LHA.EXE
```

The above command tests the LHA.EXE program.

u	update

Updates older files in an archive and adds new ones.

Example:

```
LHA u passrc
```

This command places new files in the PASSRC.LZH archive, and older versions of archived files are replaced by more current ones.

v	verbose list

Provides a detailed list of an archive's contents.

Example:

```
LHA v -x archive
```

This command works exactly the same as the ARJ command ARJ v x archive.

x	extended extract

Extracts files using complete path information. Existing directories are recreated.

222

Path information is saved in an archive only if the "-r" and "-x" options are used when compressing.

Example:

```
LHA x FUN C:\GAMES\ *.*
```

All files from the FUN archive are extracted to the GAMES directory on the hard drive. If the archive includes any subdirectories, these are automatically created under GAMES.

Options

LHA also works with options. Each switch's letter can be followed by a 0, 1, or 2. Sometimes 1 and 2 have the same meaning, in which case 2 isn't listed.

NOTE: We'll use the "-" character to designate an option. The "/" character can also be used.

-a	attributes

Designates certain attributes for files to be processed. The default setting "-a0" ignores system and hidden files.

-a0	Files with the system or hidden attributes aren't processed.
-a1	Files with special attributes (hidden and system) are processed.

Examples:

```
LHA a system -a1 *.sys
```

With the above command, all system files are compressed and placed in the SYSTEM.LZH archive.

```
LHA e system -a1 *.sys
```

The above command decompresses system files with the system and hidden attributes.

-c	ignore comparison of time stamp

Suppresses the checking of file time stamps.

Usually the "e", "f", "u", and "x" commands affect only the more current version of a file. The "-c1" option doesn't perform any date-time comparisons.

-c0	Default: Time stamps are compared.	-c1	Time stamps are ignored.

-i	ignore case

Indicates case-sensitivity.

The DOS operating system doesn't recognize the difference between upper and lowercase characters. This option applies only to systems that make this distinction.

-l	long display

Controls type of screen output.

For both compression and decompression, the "-l1" option records paths relative to the current directory. The "-l2" option inserts the directory prefix from the command line.

-l0	Show filenames only.
-l1	Show pathnames relative to working directory.
-l2	Show complete pathnames including working directory from command line.

-m	no message

Automatically answers "yes" to user queries.

With the default setting (-m0), the user must respond to a query when target files with the same name are found.

```
C:\>LHA E -M0 EXAMPLES

Extracting from archive : EXAMPLES.LZH

Skipped  CHAP03.BAK  : newer or same file exists.
Skipped  CHAP07.BAK  : newer or same file exists.
'CHAP07.DOC' Overwrite? [Y/N]
```

224

A query is also displayed for creating directories. The setting "-m1" tells the program to assume a "yes" answer and suppress the query. If you try to overwrite a write-protected file, a "file creation error" still occurs. To solve this problem, use "-m2". When extracting a file that already exists, the program assigns a unique suffix from 000 to 999.

-m0	Default: All queries must be answered manually.
-m1	All queries are automatically answered "yes".
-m2	Extracted file are automatically assigned unique names.

Examples:

```
LHA e -m1 archive
```

All files are extracted from the archive. If a file already exists and is not write-protected, the program overwrites it.

```
LHA e -m2 archive
```

As in the above example, all files are extracted. Duplicate files are assigned unique names by means of ascending numeric suffixes so nothing is overwritten.

-n	no indicator

Limits or suppresses screen output during compression. Normally a moving bar is shown with the compression rate, for example:

```
C:\>LHA E EXAMPLES

Extracting from archive : EXAMPLES.LZH

Melted    CHAP03.BAK    oooooooo
Melted    CHAP07.BAK    oooooooo
Melted    CHAP07.DOC    oooooo
Melted    CHAP05.DOC    oooooooo
Melted    CHAP04.DOC    ooooooo
Melted    CHAP03.DOC    oooooooo
Melted    CHAP01.DOC    oooooo
Melted    CHAP02.DOC    ooooo
Melted    ABACAT.DOC    o

C:\>
```

The bar is suppressed with "-n1".

To suppress all screen output (for example, when using LHA.EXE in a custom program), use "-n2".

-n0	Default: Progress bar is displayed.
-n1	Suppresses progress bar.
-n2	Suppresses progress bar and filenames.

-o	old compatible method

Selects old compression method for compatibility.

The "-o1" option selects the compression method used in LHARC Version 1.13. The file header then appears in LH113c format.

-p	distinguish full path names

Searches precisely for archived files.

If files are extracted without the "-p" option, no effort is made to determine whether duplicate filenames exist under different directories. This means you could end up extracting the wrong file or accidentally overwriting an existing file.

Examples:

```
LHA e DATES imprtant.DOC
```

This command extracts the file called "IMPRTANT.DOC" from the DATES archive. If two such files exist in the archive (suppose they are specified as OLD\IMPRTANT.DOC and IMPRTANT.DOC), both will be extracted. If you want to prevent this, use the "-p" option and specify exactly which one you want.

```
LHA e Dates -p imprtant.DOC
```

With the above command, only IMPRTANT.DOC is extracted.

-r	recurse subdirs

Allows subdirectories to be searched recursively. If you archive files from different subdirectories, you should include the "-x" option so that paths are also saved.

Examples:

```
LHA a COMPLETE -r c:\*.DOC
```

This command archives all .DOC files on the C: drive. Paths are not saved. If identical filenames are encountered, LHA displays the following error:

```
C:\>LHA A COMPLETE -R C:\*.DOC

Updating archive : COMPLETE.LZH


Same names in another path : 'CHAP07.DOC'

C:\>
```

By including pathnames in the archive, you can save multiple versions of files that have the same names.

```
LHA a COMPLETE -r-x c:\*.TXT
```

-s	skip message

Suppresses the message:

```
Extracting from archive : COMPLETE.LZH

Skipped  PAYR0112.DOC : newer or same file exists.
Skipped  PAYR1124.DOC : newer or same file exists.
Skipped  PAYR1201.DOC : newer or same file exists.
Skipped  PAYR1215.DOC : newer or same file exists.
Skipped  PAYR1229.DOC : newer or same file exists.
Skipped  VENDOR.DOC : newer or same file exists.
Skipped  CHAP07.DOC : newer or same file exists.
Skipped  CHAP05.DOC : newer or same file exists.
Skipped  CHAP04.DOC : newer or same file exists.
Skipped  CHAP03.DOC : newer or same file exists.
Skipped  CHAP01.DOC : newer or same file exists.
Skipped  CHAP02.DOC : newer or same file exists.
Skipped  README:DOC : newer or same file exists.
Skipped  SHAREWAR.DOC : newer or same file exists.
Skipped  LICENSE.DOC : newer or same file exists.
Skipped  ORDER.DOC : newer or same file exists.
Skipped  ADDENDUM.DOC : newer or same file exists.
Skipped  MANUAL.DOC : newer or same file exists.
Skipped  PAUL.DOC : newer or same file exists.
Skipped  DIETAPI.DOC : newer or same file exists.
Skipped  DIET144.DOC : newer or same file exists.

C:\>
```

-t	time stamp

Matches the time stamp of the archive to that of the archived files. This switch works with the a, d, f, m, and u commands.

-t0	Default: The archive is stamped with the current system time.
-t1	The archive is stamped with the time of the most current file in the archive.

Examples:

```
LHA a Now
```

The program compresses all files from the current directory to the Now archive. The time stamp is the current system time.

```
LHA a -t1 now
```

This command is similar to the previous example, except that the archive takes its time stamp from the most current file saved.

-w	work directory

Defines a work directory where the program temporarily stores information for managing the archiving/extraction process.

The data is assembled first in the work area and then copied to the target medium. After the process is successfully completed, the temporary file space is released. This technique is used for faster processing.

Example:

```
LHA a -we:\ archive *.TXT
```

The .TXT files are temporarily stored on a RAM disk in drive E:, then copied to a diskette in drive A:.

-x	extended names

Archives pathname with file.

This is required, along with the recursion option "-r", if you want to later perform an extended extract ("x" command) to restore the complete directory structure.

Examples:

```
LHA a -x texts c:\word5\book.TXT
```

The BOOK.TXT file is archived along with its complete path.

228

```
LHA a texts -r-x c:\word5
```

All files in the WORD5 directory and its subdirectories are archived along with complete paths.

-z	zero compression

Saves files without compressing them. Normally all files specified are compressed. This corresponds to the setting "-z0."

-z0	Default: All files are compressed.
-z1	No files are compressed.
-z2	Files ending in ARC, LZH, LZS, PAK, ZIP or ZOO are not compressed.
-zXX	Files ending in XXX are not compressed.

If you don't want to compress files other than the types listed, specify the appropriate endings. Remember that ARJ isn't included among the listed types.

Examples:

```
LHA a -z1 texts *.TXT
```

None of the files selected should be compressed.

```
LHA a -zdbf dbase *.*
```

All dBase (.DBF) files are placed in the DBASE.LZH archive without compression.

```
LHA a D:Backup C:\ -r-x -z2 -zARJ -zGIF
```

All files present on the C: drive are saved to the BACKUP archive on drive D:. Files ending in ARC, LZH, LZS, PAK, ZIP, ZOO, ARJ, and GIF are saved as is, since they already are in compressed form.

/-	first letter switch

Considers the first character of a file specification to be part of the normal filename.

LHA sometimes gives a special interpretation to the first character of a filename. The prefix "@" is used to indicate a file that contains instructions for LHA. Such a file is read and interpreted as a sequence of command lines, rather than being archived.

229

If you want to archive a file whose name begins with "@", use "/-1."

With the "-2" setting, LHA will also recognize "-" as the first character of a filename. The switch is deactivated by typing: "-[0]".

/-1	Treat initial "@" as part of normal filename.
/-2	Treat initial "@" or "-" as part of normal filename.
/-[0]	Deactivate first two options.

ERRORLEVELS

The following table shows the error codes that LHA can return in the ERRORLEVEL variable. You can check the value of ERRORLEVEL in a batch file.

Code	Meaning
0	No error
1	Possible CRC failure in connection with a "t", "x" or "e" command. Other possibilities include insufficient disk space or file already exists.
2	Fatal error, not processed.
3	Temporary archive could not be converted.

On error level 3, the temporary archive remains in the work directory under the name "LHTEMP)2(.LZH". You can salvage your work by renaming this file and saving it as a normal archive.

PKZIP/PKUNZIP 2.04g Commands

We'll discuss the PKZip and PKUnzip programs in the same section because they use essentially the same commands. If a command applies to only one of these commands, this is indicated in the heading.

Syntax for PKZIP

```
PKZIP [-b[path]] [options] Zipfile [@list] [files...]
```

230

Syntax for PKUNZIP

```
PKUNZIP [options] Zipfile [drive:path\] [file...]
```

Commands

PKZIP -a	add

Adds files to the specified archive. If a file already exists, it is overwritten. If the archive does not exist, it is created.

Examples:

```
PKZIP a archive
```

This command compresses all files from the current drive and directory to the archive called "ARCHIVE.ZIP."

```
PKZIP a e:\pics\graphic c:\windows\*.bmp
```

This command compresses all .BMP files under the WINDOWS directory on drive C: to an archive called "GRAPHIC.ZIP", under the PICS directory on drive E:.

PKZIP -b	working directory

Designates a temporary working directory on another drive. This is helpful when you're archiving to diskettes or when you have a large RAM drive available to speed up processing.

Files are archived first to the temporary area and then copied to the target drive and directory. When the process is successfully completed, the temporary archive is released. This usually increases compression speed.

Example:

```
PKZIP a -b e:\ a:\archive *.TXT
```

All .TXT files are temporarily compressed to a RAM disk on drive E: and then copied to a diskette in drive A:. If the process is interrupted, both the temporary and the permanent archive are deleted.

231

PKZIP -c	comment 1

Assigns a comment of up to 60 characters to a compressed file.

 The comment is entered in dialog mode and terminated by pressing `Enter`.

Examples:

```
PKZIP a -c texts *.TXT
```

The user is prompted to enter a comment for each file to be compressed.

```
PKZIP -C     comment 2
```

Only updated files receive a comment.

```
PKUNZIP -c   screen extract
```

The contents of a specified compressed file are displayed on the screen. If a file isn't specified, every file on the archive is displayed. The additional use of the "m" option pauses the screen when it is full.

-cm	Stops after every full screen.

PKZIP -d	delete

Deletes one or more files from an archive.

Example:

```
PKZIP d archive *.TXT junk.DOC
```

All files ending in .TXT and the file named "JUNK.DOC" are deleted from the archive.

PKUNZIP -d	create directory

Automatically creates missing directories during decompression.

This command is only useful if the archive was compressed using the "-r" and "-p/P" options.

232

Example:

PKUNZIP -d complete C:\TEMP\

With the above command, the COMPLETE archive is extracted to C:\TEMP. If COMPLETE contains subdirectories, they are automatically created when necessary.

PKZIP -e	extra compression method

Selects the compression method to be used. A second letter identifies the desired method. The following options are available:

-ea	Imploding is used for all ASCII files, and shrinking is used for all binary files.
-eb	Imploding is used for all binary files, and shrinking is used for all ASCII files.
-es	Shrinking is used for all files. This is usually the fastest method.
-ex	Imploding is used for all files. This is the default method.

Shrinking is slightly faster but less thorough than imploding. Imploding, a slower but more compact compression, is the default setting.

PKUNZIP -e	extract order

Determines the extraction sequence for archived files.

You do not have to extract files in the same sequence in which they were archived. A second letter gives the desired sort criterion (order is always ascending).

-ec	By CRC code.	-en	By filename.
-ed	By time stamp.	-ep	By compression rate.
-ee	By file extension.	-es	By size.

Parameters can be combined.

Example:

```
PKUNZIP -eend BACKUP
```

This command decompresses the file to the current directory. Files are accessed by extension (e), name (n), and date-time (d).

PKZIP, PKUNZIP -f	freshen

Freshens an archive. Archived files are replaced by more current versions.

Example:

```
PKZIP -f -r document *.TXT *.DOC
```

With the above command, the DOCUMENT archive is freshened with all .TXT and .DOC files in the current directory and its underlying subdirectories.

The same command in PKUNZIP extracts only files already present in an older version in the target directory.

PKZIP, PKUNZIP -h	help

Displays the help screen.

PKZIP -i	backup

Archives only files with the archive attribute set.

Once a file has been archived, its bit is cleared. If the same command is immediately repeated, files won't be saved.

Example:

```
PKZIP -i backup c:\*.TXT -r
```

All .TXT files carrying the archive attribute are compressed to the BACKUP.ZIP archive.

PKZIP, PKUNZIP -j	include attributes

Allows attributes to be used for file selection.

-jh	Select hidden files.	-jh	Select system files.
-jr	Select write-protected (read-only) files.		

Any combination of attributes is also allowed.

234

Example:

```
PKZIP -a -jhsr MAIN C:\*.* D:\*.*
```

This command archives all files in the root directories of the C: and D: drives. System, hidden, and read-only files like MSDOS.SYS and IO.SYS are included.

-J	exclude attributes

Works like the "-j" switch, but specifies types of files to exclude from an archive. Be sure to observe the proper case to obtain the desired result.

Examples:

```
PKZIP -jhs system *.sys
```

This command compresses all .SYS files, including hidden and system files, to the SYSTEM.ZIP archive.

```
PKZIP -Jr -jsh texts *.TXT
```

All .TXT files that are not write-protected are compressed.

PKZIP -k	keep original date

Keeps the same time stamp when an archive is updated.

Example:

```
PKZIP -f -k archive
```

The date-time on the archive isn't changed when files are rearchived to it.

-l	license

Shows terms of PKZIP license on the screen.

PKZIP -m	move

Places files in the specified archive and deletes the original versions. Deleting doesn't occur until compression and archiving are complete.

Normally Move, like Add, overwrites already-archived files. There are two parameters for changing this, however.

-m	Normal Move.
-mf	Moves only files already in the archive as older versions.
-mu	Same as above, but also includes files not yet present in the archive.

Example:

```
PKZIP -m dbase *.dbf
```

All dBase files are packed to a new archive called "DBASE.ZIP", and their originals are deleted.

PKUNZIP -n only newer

Extracts only files newer than those on the original disk.

This is a safety feature that prevents accidentally destroying the most current version of a file. Files not present in the target directory are always extracted.

Example:

```
pkunzip -n texts c:\word5\
```

All files in the TEXTS archive are extracted to the WORD5 directory on the C: drive, unless a more current version already exists there.

PKZIP -o time stamp of oldest file

Assigns the time stamp of the oldest archived file to the archive.

The default procedure is to stamp the archive with the current date-time.

Example:

```
PKZIP -a -o Old *.TXT
```

PKUNZIP -o overwrite

Files with the same names in the target directory are automatically overwritten.

Example:

```
PKUNZIP -o-d GAMES C:\
```

236

This command overwrites any like-named files in the target directory with the extracted version. This is rather dangerous, especially in the root directory. The "-d" switch creates any missing directories.

PKZIP -p	store pathnames

Stores pathnames along with archived files. You must do this if you use the recursion switch to archive multiple directories.

-p	Saves pathnames relative to current directory.
-P	Saves complete path including portion from command line.

Examples:

```
PKZIP -a TEXTS -r -p \WORD\*.TXT
```

Assuming that the current directory is \WORD, this variant will add path information to the archive only for files taken from subdirectories under \WORD.

```
PKZIP -a TEXTS -r -P \WORD\*.TXT
```

This variant stores the complete path information, including the \WORD directory, for every file archived.

PKUNZIP -p	print

Sends file contents to a printer. Available options are:

-p	Contents are sent to printer (default).
-pa	Contents are sent to printer in ASCII format.
-pb	Contents are sent to printer in binary format.
pc	Specifies serial interface as printer port.
pn	Identifies serial interface to be used (i.e., COM1). Otherwise assumes standard.

Example:

```
PKUNZIP -pbc2 pics
```

Archived files (presumably graphics) are sent over COM2 to the printer.

PKZIP -r	recurse subdirs

Subdirectories are recursed during processing.

Any commands that access subdirectories should include the "-p/P" switch to distinguish like-named files.

Example:

```
PKZIP -a -r secure c:\*.bak
```

All backup (.BAK) files in the root and underlying directories of the C: drive are packed to the SECURE.ZIP archive.

-s	scramble with password

Applies a password to an archived file.

A password is case-sensitive. It follows the "-s" switch directly, with no space separator. A file archived with a password can only be extracted by entering the same password again.

Example:

```
PKZIP -a secret -sJoshua
```

All new files archived to SECRET.ZIP are given the password "Joshua."

PKUNZIP -t	test zipfile

Checks an archive for data integrity.

Example:

```
PKUNZIP -t archive
```

With this command, archive is tested for errors.

PKZIP -u	update

Adds new files to an archive and updates existing ones that have older time stamps.

238

Example:

```
PKZIP -u passcr
```

Adds new files to the PASSCR.ZIP archive. Also updates files already present if a newer version is available.

-v	view archive

Displays archive contents according to certain criteria. A letter may follow the "-v" to indicate criteria desired.

-v	All information.
-vb	Brief format; all information except CRC value and file attributes.
-vt	Technical format; additional information for each file.
-vc	Comments.
-vd	Sort by date.
-ve	Sort by extension.
-vn	Sort by name.
-vo	Sort by order within archive.
-vp	Sort by percent compression.
-vs	Sort by size.
-vr	Reverse sort sequence.

Parameters can be combined.

Example:

```
PKZIP -vbenr COMPLETE
```

This command shows the contents of the COMPLETE archive in brief format, sorted by descending extension/name.

-x	exclude

Excludes specified files from processing.

Examples:

```
PKZIP -a texts *.TXT -xprivate.TXT
```

All .TXT files except PRIVATE.TXT are archived.

```
PKZIP -d texts *.TXT -xsecret.TXT -xprivat.TXT
```

All .TXT files in the TEXTS archive, except for PRIVATE and SECRET, are deleted.

-z	zipfile comment

Queries the user for an archive comment. Entry is in dialog mode. This can also be used to change an existing comment.

ERRORLEVELs in PKZIP

The following table shows the error codes that can be returned by PKZIP.

Code	Error
0	No error.
1	Incorrect filename.
2,3	Error in archive.
4-11	Insufficient memory.
12	No files found to archive or delete.
13	Archive or list file not found.
14	Disk is full.
15	Archive is write-protected.
16	Incorrect parameter in command line.
17	Too many files to process.

ERRORLEVELs in PKUNZIP

The following table shows the error codes that can be returned by PKUNZIP.

Code	Meaning	Code	Meaning
0	No error.	10	Incorrect parameter in command line.
1	Warning (e.g., CRC failure).	11	No files found to extract or view.
2,3	Error in archive.	50	Disk is full.
4-8	Insufficient memory.	51	Defective archive, unable to extract.
9	File not found.		

ZOO Commands

Syntax

ZOO is the only program that has two completely different syntaxes. One is the novice user syntax:

```
ZOO -Cmd archive[.ZOO] file...
```

This syntax contains commands that are abbreviations, which are easily identified. The other syntax is the expert syntax. We'll describe this in detail, because there are so many combinations and ZOO isn't as widely used as the other programs.

```
ZOO {acfDeghlLPTuUvx}[aAcCdEfImMnNoOpPqu1:/.@n] archive file...
```

Commands

-add

Adds new files to an archive. Overwrites existing files and creates archive if necessary.

Examples:

```
ZOO -add archive
```

241

This command compresses all files in the current drive and directory to the ARCHIVE.ZOO archive.

```
ZOO -add Games *.exe *.dos *.com
```

The above command compresses all EXE, DOS, and COM files in the current drive and directory to the GAMES archive.

-comment

Adds comments of up to 64K characters to an existing archived file.

To terminate the entry, type "/END" on a separate line. Then the comments for the next file can be entered. Both filenames and wildcards are allowed.

Remember that comments lower the compression rate, especially on small files, because they are not compressed.

Example:

```
ZOO -comment batch autoexec.bat word5.bat
```

With the above command, you'll be asked to enter comments for the two files AUTOEXEC.BAT and WORD5.BAT in the BATCH.ZOO archive.

-delete

Deletes specified files from an archive.

Example:

```
ZOO -delete archive *.TXT
```

All .TXT files are deleted from the archive.

-extract

Extracts one or more files from a specified archive to the current directory or other specified target directory.

If filenames or wildcards aren't specified, all files in the archive are decompressed. Overwriting occurs only for older versions in the target directory, after confirmation from the user.

242

Example:

```
ZOO -extract archive
```

All files in the ARCHIVE.ZOO archive are decompressed to the current directory.

-freshen

Freshens (updates) an archive by replacing older compressed versions with newer ones. Files not already present aren't added.

-list

Displays the contents of the specified archive on the screen.

Files are listed in the order in which they were compressed (alphabetically). Other sort criteria aren't allowed.

-move

Moves a new file to the specified archive and deletes the original. Deleting takes place only after the file is successfully compressed and archived.

Example:

```
ZOO- move dbase *.dbf
```

All dBASE files in the current directory are compressed to the DBASE.ZOO archive. The original files are then deleted.

-print

Prints the contents of an archive to the standard output device. Normally this is the screen. Output can also be directed to other devices, such as printers (see your DOS manual).

Example:

```
ZOO -print archive >prn
```

The contents of all files compressed in the ARCHIVE.ZOO archive are output to the printer.

-test

Tests the integrity of an archive. If filenames or wildcards aren't specified, every archived file is tested for error-free compression.

Example:

```
ZOO -test imprtant
```

All files in the IMPRTANT.ZOO archive are tested for error-free compression.

-update

Updates older versions of archived files and adds files not present.

Example:

```
ZOO -update passcr
```

New files are added to the PASSCR.ZOO archive, and existing versions are updated if newer versions are found.

ERRORLEVELS

ZOO is very stingy with error codes returned to the operating system. Therefore, you can only determine whether the execution was error-free.

Code	Meaning
0	No error
1	Error during execution

Installing The Companion CD-ROM

Installing In Windows 3.x Or Windows For Workgroups

Our goal is to make installing the contents of your ZIP BIBLE companion CD-ROM a simple process. We'll use step-by-step instructions in this chapter to explain how to install the companion CD-ROM.

The steps to install the companion CD-ROM in Windows 3.x or Windows for Workgroups are identical.

Before continuing, you must have Windows running. Make certain the Program Manager desktop appears on your screen. If necessary, double-click the Program Manager icon to display the Program Manager.

Follow these steps to install the companion CD-ROM in Windows 3.x or Windows for Workgroups.

1. Insert the companion CD-ROM in your CD drive.

2. Move the mouse pointer to the menu bar in the Program Manager.

3. Click **File** to open the **File** menu (see the following illustration).

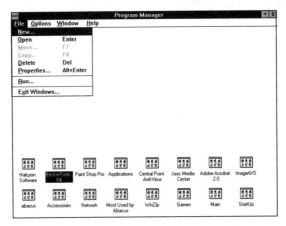

4. Select the **Run...** command from the **File** menu. This opens the Run dialog box.

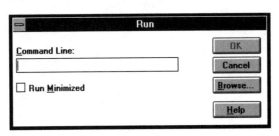

5. Type the following in the "Command Line:" text box:

    ```
    D:\MENU.EXE
    ```

    We're assuming your CD-ROM is drive D: otherwise change that letter to correspond to your CD-ROM drive letter. The Run dialog box should appear like the following illustration:

    If so, click the ⌈OK⌋ button.

6. The "ZIP BIBLE" will soon appear on your screen.

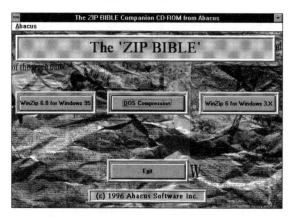

7. Click the WinZip 6 for Windows 3.x button to install WinZip 6.0.

8. Click the Niko Mak Computing WinZip 6.0 button.

This starts the installation program for WinZip 6.0. Follow the prompts and instructions on the screen to complete the installation.

Installing In Windows 95

Microsoft's Windows 95 has a new CD-ROM drive feature. When you insert a CD-ROM into your drive, Windows 95 will load the 'loader' program for you. We've already done this for you on the companion CD-ROM. Therefore, you won't need to type anything for the ZIP BIBLE Menu program to run for you.

Alternatively, you can install the companion CD-ROM by following these step-by-step instructions:

1. Make certain you're at the Windows 95 desktop. Your screen should look similar to the following illustration.

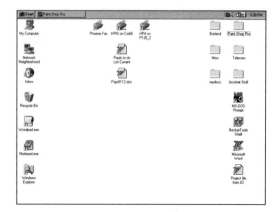

2. Click the **Start** button. Select the **Run...** icon command near the bottom of the Windows 95 icon list. This opens the Run dialog box.

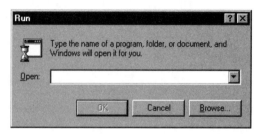

3. Enter the CD-ROM drive letter designation and program name ("menu") in the "Open:" text box. For example, type the following:

```
d:\menu
```

and press ⟨Enter⟩. We're assuming your CD-ROM is drive D:, otherwise change that letter to correspond to your CD-ROM drive letter. The Run dialog box should appear like the following illustration:

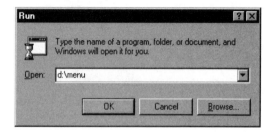

If so, click the ⟨OK⟩ button.

6. The "ZIP BIBLE" opening window will soon appear on your screen.

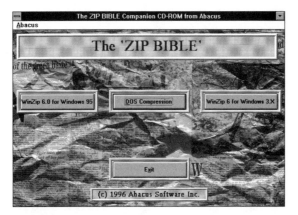

7. Click the ⌈WinZip 6.0 for Windows 95⌉ button to install WinZip 95.

8. Click the ⌈Niko Mak Computing WinZip 95⌉ button.

This starts the installation program for WinZip 95. Follow the prompts and instructions on the screen to complete the installation.

DOS Compression

Here you'll find a collection of DOS-based shareware data compression programs. The most popular is PKZIP. You must use all these utilities from the DOS prompt.

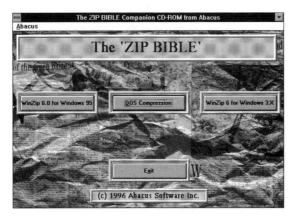

Installation through Windows

Follow the step-by-step instructions in this chapter concerning installing the CD-ROM in either Windows 3.x or Windows 95.

Click the DOS Compression button. This will open the Installing DOS 'Zip' Utilities dialog box. Click on the Install PKZip, LHArc, Zoo, Diet and Arj button. This will start the DOS Compression Utilities installation program.

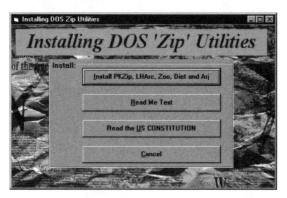

Follow the instructions on the screen to complete the installation.

Installation through the DOS prompt

To install from the DOS prompt, switch to your CD-ROM drive. Type the following at the DOS prompt:

```
INSTALL
```

Press the Enter key.

This will start the DOS Compression Utilities installation. Follow the instructions on the screen to complete the installation.

250

Glossary Of Terms

10

Algorithms

Algorithms are instructions to the computer, telling it to solve a problem in a specific, predetermined manner. Data compression programs use algorithms to determine how data is compressed. Many data compression programs use the well-known Huffman algorithm.

Most data compression programs don't include a glossary defining the most important terms. So, we'll define several terms in this chapter that used in data compression.

ANSI

American National Standards Institute. ANSI is standard for interpreting codes and characters.

Archive

An archive is a file created by a data compression program. It's used for storing other files. An archive can contain several files that can be compressed.

Archive bit

This bit is one of the attributes that every file has. The archive bit indicates whether a file has been changed since the last time it was saved. Data compression programs can check this bit to determine whether to backup the file. Other file attributes are hidden, system or read-only.

ASCII

Standard that assigns characters different codes from 0 to 255. ASCII is an abbreviation for American Standard Code for Information Interchange.

Bit

The smallest unit of information on a computer is called a bit. A bit can only be 0 or 1 in value.

Cache program

A program that places data in temporary storage. This speeds up access to this data. Software cache programs that go back and forth from the hard drive to RAM are very common. When RAM accesses the hard drive, the cache program can often provide the data from temporary storage. This is much faster than accessing the data from the hard drive.

CRC-Code

Abbreviation for Cyclic Redundancy Check. As a safety precaution, after a program archives files, these files receive a code calculated from the compressed data. During a test or decompression, the code is recalculated. The file is damaged and cannot be decompressed if any differences between the current calculation and the old CRC code are found.

Downwardly compatible

Programs that are able to process data from earlier program versions. Some compression programs have switches for choosing compatible methods in data compression.

File attributes

File attributes are information about the status of a file. The following attributes are possible: Hidden, System, Archive, and Read-only.

Garble

Garble is a technical term for archiving with a password.

Header

File header with important information about a file. Archives have an archive header and local headers, which contain information about the individual archived files.

Hidden

File attribute. When this attribute is set, the file cannot be displayed at the DOS prompt with the DIR command.

Huffman

Developed the Huffman algorithm for compressing files.

IBM graphic character set

All characters with ASCII codes 128 to 255 are called IBM graphic characters (or the extended graphic character set). The IBM graphic character set includes foreign characters.

Command line

Another word for the DOS prompt is the command line. If you aren't running Windows, you enter all your commands and run programs from this line.

Critical error messages

Errors that usually cause the PC system to crash. The following is a typical critical error message:

LZW

LZW is an abbreviation for the developers of a data compression algorithm: Lempel, Ziv and Welch.

Manual

The file containing the manual for your data compression program is also called the manual

Masking

A process for determining whether a specific bit is set.

Module

A module is a part of a program or program system. If you make an SFX archive from a normal program, then you add a module to the archive that is in charge of decompressing the actual archive.

Multiple-Volume

An archive that's located on more than one diskette.

Options

An option is an alternative that modifies a command in a specific manner. In this book, this term is used interchangeably with parameter or switch.

Parameter

See Options.

Progress Bar

A progress bar indicates how much of a job is already completed.

Ratio

The relationship of the original size and the compressed size of a file. Different compression programs treat the ratio differently. Some indicate the percentage by which the compressed file is smaller than the original size, while others indicate the percentage the file has been reduced to.

Switch

See Options.

SFX

Abbreviation for self-extracting archive. This is an archive with a program module that decompresses the data of the archive. A separate compression program is no longer necessary to restore the data.

System file

A system file is a file whose System attribute is set.

Text file

A file containing only readable information.

Time Stamps

Every file has a date and time on which it was created or last changed. This is referred to as a time stamp.

Verbose List

Data compression term for a detailed list of the contents of an archive.

Volume

Refers to a diskette or hard drive.

Volume Label

Name of a diskette or hard drive (Volume).

Index

D

Multimedia Presentation

PC Photography Book

The PC Photography Book is for all camera buffs, home users, hobbyists, desktop publishers, graphic artists, marketing communication professionals and multimedia enthusiasts.

Many companies, including Kodak, Seattle Film Works, Storm Software, Delrina, Hewlett-Packard and others, are pioneering a new consumer level technology which lets you move common photos or snap shots onto your PC. Digital imaging software and graphic gear is easier to use, more affordable and the quality of output excellent.

PC Photography starts with the basics of image processing and taking quality photos. A special treatment is given to Kodak's photo CD format that allows anyone to put photos on CD-ROM. The technology and process are both explained in depth. It then moves on to examine how today's hardware and software work—both the digital camera and the photo reader.

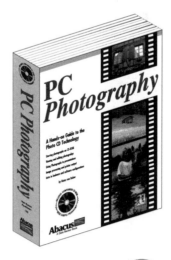

Includes CD-ROM with Sample Programs

Learn how to work with: Micrografx PhotoMagic, Microsoft Publisher, CorelDraw, Aldus Freehand and Photostyler, and Adobe PhotoShop.

The companion CD-ROM includes samplers of:

- Toshiba's Photo/Graphic Viewer
- MicroTek's Photo Star graphic utility
- PCD photo examples used in the book
- Collection of popular shareware graphics utilities including:
    - JASC'S PaintShop Pro
    - Graphics WorkShop
- Several industry standard Phillips CD-I software drivers

Author: Heinz von Buelow and Dirk Paulissen
Order Item: #B293
ISBN: 1-55755-293-2

SRP: $34.95 US/$46.95 CAN includes CD-ROM

To order direct call Toll Free 1-800-451-4319

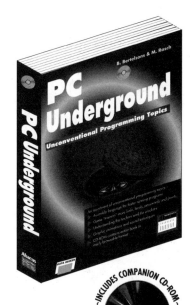

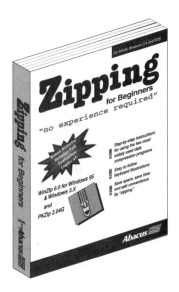